'OKER' ABORIGINAL HITMAN

THE STORY OF CHARLES FREDERICK QUINLAN, 1980'S AUSTRALIA'S MOST WANTED MAN

BRIDGET NEZAR

Cataloguing in Publication Data:
TITLE: 'Oker' - Aboriginal Hitman
AUTHOR: Bridget Nezar
FORMATTING & PUBLISHING: KJS Publishing

CONTENTS

AUTHOR'S NOTE

The big black man stood up hesitantly. He looked uncomfortable standing behind the church lectern. Although he mumbled as he searched for the right words, his story was riveting.

As I listened I thought, "If what this man is saying is true, someone should write his story."

At the end of the school term six glorious weeks of holidays stretched before me; a good time to start writing the story of Charles Frederick Quinlan, an Aboriginal man who was once one of Australia's most wanted men.

Initially I thought to simply record the stories of his life, the exciting escapades with the police, his eventual capture, incarceration and final release from prison. However as Charlie and I talked about his experiences and as I interviewed family and acquaintances so much more emerged. Consequently this book is more than the life of Charlie Quinlan; it is the life and experiences of the Indigenous people of the Bellbrook area from white occupation and their battle to fit into a society that was and is still non-accepting of traditional Aboriginal society and values.

Charles Frederick Quinlan sharing his testimony in church.

1

———

TIP-OFF

My mum, Judith Quinlan, lived in a rented house in Gordon Street, Port Macquarie, near the TAFE College. She never knew when I might visit. With police watching her house it wasn't safe. Over and over again police would come into her home, ransack the house and leave her belongings all over the place. It wasn't right. My mum was a respectable lady, serving her community well. She looked after kids in the street, feeding them, even giving them a bed and she had never been in trouble with the law; she didn't even drink or smoke. She was treated like a criminal because of me, her eldest son Charlie, her beloved Charlie named after her own father whom she adored. But now her father was dead, her husband was dead and I was one of Australia's most wanted men. No, it wasn't safe for me at mum's place. Nevertheless sometimes my younger brother, Ralph, and I would tap on the window at night and mum would get us some tucker. Today, I really only wanted a quick chat.

As it turned out when I was in the house sounds of sirens shattered the peaceful neighbourhood. Someone must have tipped off the cops. Not family, I could always trust my family. Mum wasn't in the house at the time. She was getting fuel with her second son, Darren, when the police cars sped past them, five, ten, twenty - she lost count. Suddenly one of the cars screeched to a halt in front on mum's car. A policeman jumped out and grabbed Darren. "What do you think you are doing?" Darren yelled with his hands in front of his face trying to protect himself. "I'm not Charlie. I don't even look like him."

The policeman, realising his mistake, spun around without a word of apology and sped off. It was always like that. Police thought they could treat us Aboriginals any way they liked and there was nothing we could do about it.

Mum got in her own vehicle and followed at a safe distance. The police vehicles were all stopped in a paddock, the back paddock of the West Port Public School and in the middle of the paddock was a shed. The police were busy putting on bullet-proof vests and arming themselves with pump-action shotguns.

"My God, they're going to kill him," she thought. Looking around she recognised Detective Williams, the head man. "Please Sir," she begged, "if you think my son is in that shed let me talk to him. I can persuade him to come out. Please don't shoot. Please let me talk to him."

"Look, Mrs. Quinlan," the Detective replied with a grin, "go home, put your feet up and have a cup of coffee."

"Heartless," Judith thought, "they're really going to kill my boy."

Dropping to her knees she prayed silently, "God, please protect my son, protect him from his enemies. You are a powerful God. There's nothing You can't do and we need You."

Before her prayer was finished a message came over the police radio, loud and clear, right from the car next to hers. "We've just seen Charlie Quinlan in a red car heading towards Kempsey," the unseen voice announced.

All was confusion. How could this be?

In seconds the police cars sped off until all the was left was a cloud of dust and a dazed Judith still on her knees whispering, "Praise God, thank you Lord, I don't know how You did that, but thank you, thank you."

I didn't believe God had anything to do with it. I was in mum's house when the police knocked on the door. My brother Ralph warned me. We actually looked alike so we planned in an emergency to take off in different directions hoping the police would follow the wrong man. So Ralph climbed out a side window while I left by a window at the back of the house, armed with two pistols. My daughter, Amanda, was playing with a hose in the backyard. I had no choice but to run past her.

I saw Detective Williams run up the side of the house yelling, "Stop, stop!"

Then he fired smashing a hole in the back fence of the yard.

As a leapt the fence I heard another volley then I felt it, pellets from a shotgun in my back and neck. Amanda stood frozen. How dare he fire near my Mandy. I hardly felt the pain I was so angry. As I fell to the ground I twisted my body around and fired 6 shots at Williams but all of them missed. I wished him dead. Adrenaline pumping I ran for cover, dodging around parked cars and into the paddock belonging to the West Port Public School. This paddock was used by the school for growing vegetables and in the middle was a shed. It was still early and the school wasn't open yet but the shed was. I went straight in and without pausing out the back door, through the high grass and into a cul-de-sac. I could hear the sirens blaring again as the police surrounded the shed.

I paused, considering what to do next. In front of me was a maroon Mazda station wagon. One look told me it was unlocked and unbelievably there were keys in the ignition and the engine running. There was no-one in sight so I quickly got into the driver's seat and headed for the highway.

"I've got a bit of time," I thought to myself. "The coppers think I'm in the shed and they don't know this car is stolen yet."

Not wanting to draw attention to myself I kept to the speed limit. There were police everywhere. I must have passed about thirty squad cars on the highway. I learn later there had been a shoot-out at Nambucca and the policemen were driving back to Port Macquarie but no-one realised they were passing the notorious criminal, Charlie Quinlan.

I drove as far as the bridge crossing the Macleay River at Kempsey when a paddy wagon spun around to chase me. Word must have got out about the stolen car. I gunned the Mazda round the corner, 70 mph, two wheels in the air and two on the median strip. I had learnt in prison the best way to escape was to back-tail so I drove around the block and started to follow the paddy wagon. Now Kempsey was my back yard. I knew all the streets and had a lot of relatives living there. As the paddy wagon continued on the highway west I turned off the highway and drove to my Auntie's place at Sea Street. By this time I was feeling faint from loss of blood and car seat was covered in blood.

I was tired and so, so thirsty. I parked the car down the side of the house where it could not be seen from the road. A little girl was playing in the yard. Curiously she came to the driver's side of the car.

"Water, water," I whispered.

The girl turned on the hose spraying the water through the open window. That woke me up. I took the hose and hosed myself off, while drinking deeply in great gulps. Thinking more clearly now I drove to a cousin's place and parked the car in the garage.

"Get yourself into a shower and clean up,"my cousin hissed, I'll watch the road."

It really was a miraculous escape. How had the police missed me in the grass? Who would leave a car just in the right place with the key in the ignition? Funny thing, I never did get charged for stealing that car! If I'd been thinking straight, I might have been thankful to God for preserving my life, but I wasn't thinking straight. I was just angry, angry at the police, angry at the white man's world and I was exhausted from the chase.

I slept and woke about 3 in the morning. I had to get out of Kempsey. I drove the car down North Street. By know I knew roadblocks would be set up so when I reached the railway line I eased the car onto the lines and drove along the tracks almost to Macksville. As I approached

Macksville I saw a roadblock in the distance so I turned around and headed for a familiar place, a swamp, and reeving up I drove the Mazda straight into it. Before the car sank I climbed out the window onto the roof and sat right there until the car was fully submerged. Three times police passed that swamp but I was hidden in the mud and they never saw me.

Vanessa Kennedy's reported the drama in the Macleay Argus Thursday November 17, 1988 as follows:

Police search for armed man after high speed chase:

Police continued to search late yesterday afternoon for a man described as armed and dangerous after Tuesday's wild car chase through the streets of Kempsey. Security is so tight police refuse to give details of the man or their search. However an alert has gone out to all the Mid North Coast stations with instructions to remain silent.

A maroon Mazda station wagon driven by a large Aboriginal man took the traffic light intersection on two wheels with police on his tail. Eyewitnesses saw a red or maroon Mazda station wagon, followed by a heavy F-100 Paddy wagon, race across the traffic bridge and circle the central business district.

The drama began at Port Macquarie, where two carloads of Kempsey police had been called to help surround an old house between Westport High and primary schools. Police had gone to question the man but would not say why. Minutes later the men fled through a back window and carrying a rifle ran across the Oxley Highway to the primary school. Police feared the man would take a number of children hostage and called for reinforcements.

A search of surrounding bushland and streets was made before an on-the-spot report of a vehicle being stolen sent police racing back towards Kempsey. Half an hour later a patrolling police vehicle sighted the man driving into Kempsey and followed.

With the lights at green, the Mazda raced over the traffic bridge, corned on two wheels in front of Barsby's, accelerated up Smith Street, turning abruptly into Forth Street. Smith Street shoppers could hear the squeal of tyres and sirens before the vehicle reappeared suddenly from Forth Street. They turned right dodged traffic along Smith Street dodging traffic as they switched lanes before screaming into the RSL carpark and under the traffic bridge. The cars clocked more than 100km per hour down Belgrave Street to West Kempsey. Police lost the Mazda in River Street.

Police have released a description of the man and warn people not to approach him. He is described as Aboriginal, of solid build and about 26-years of age. He has black curly hair and brown eye and was last seen wearing a yellow singlet top.

Anyone seeing this man is urged to call their nearest police station urgently.

Not all the details were correct. The incident at West Port Primary School took place early in the morning when there were no children at the school. The idea of me taking children as hostages was either poor reporting or a fabrication to buy public sympathy.

The Port Macquarie News Wednesday November 16, 1988 also reported the search for me. It was an accurate description of the event including the report that officers were searching with weapons drawn as my mother, Judith, described in her account.

Police search for armed escapee

Police with guns drawn searched an area of Westport yesterday afternoon for a man who had earlier escaped from police custody.

Port Macquarie police were assisted by police officers from Wauchope and Kempsey in the search for the armed man.

The man was sighted at several locations in the Westport area, including Westport primary and high schools and a local house.

Police said they believed the man had stolen a car and was on his way to Kempsey late yesterday. That car was later sighted by Kempsey police.

The incident began early yesterday afternoon when Port Macquarie police went to the man's mother's house in Douglas Street, Port Macquarie.

It is believed he dived through a closed window at the rear of the house to escape.

The man's brother, who was with him at the time of the escape, was taken to the Port Macquarie Police Station for questioning.

Police in yesterday's search.

On foot now, I ran, jogging some then walking, keeping close to the mountains and avoiding the roads, right up to Bellbrook. On the way I visited my grandmother. She mixed some clay and sand with stinging nettle and plastered the mixture on my wounds. That numbed the pain and stopped the bleeding. With all the exertion two pellets had worked their way out of my back but seven remained. As I passed the Bellbrook Reserve, I was hurting and hungry but determined. This was my territory. I was heading for my camp, my safe haven, a cave at Lower Creek known only to my brother Ralph and myself.

2

HIDING PLACE

I was twenty-three years old when I discovered the cave. I only trusted my brother Ralph with its location. The cave would be a historical site if it were commonly known. Its walls were covered with ancient Aboriginal paintings, hand stencils in oranges and reds, drawing of turtles, people spearing fish or sitting around. One of my favourites was an image of a mountain, Barralbarayi, with what appeared to be red flames spirting out of its peak. Barralbarayi is the Dunghutti name for Anderson's Sugarloaf and has special significance as a place where men would take boys for initiation into manhood. The women had there own sacred places and were not allowed to walk on this mountain.

The cave was over 20 metres long. Ralph and I had fitted it out as if we were preparing for a world war. AK17s, very manageable assault rifles, M16s, rocket launchers and hand grenades made up the armoury. Many of the weapons had come from Holsworthy Army base in Sydney. I'd worked there as a trainee diesel mechanic. The weapons were not stolen exactly; they were being thrown out, discarded by the army. Some other goods were bought, mostly stolen. Sleeping bags, clothes, camouflage gear, knives, machetes and canned food were neatly stacked in the cave out of site of any air surveillance, as indeed was the cave itself. It was disguised by overgrown vegetation. That's why no-one had ever found it before us.

The coup de grace was the high powered walkie talkies with which I could contact Ralph as well as scanners which could pick up helicopter and police frequencies. Police frequencies were the easiest to detect. While the police were sending messages to helicopters and police cars, Ralph and I were listening in on their conversations. The police regarded me as a 'boong' from the bush, big but essentially uneducated, stupid in their thinking and it suited me to keep that perception alive. On the other hand I found the cops ignorant. They didn't understand my people at all. It was true I didn't write well but I could outlast any one of them in the bush. In my mind that was education that meant something.

I holed up in the cave for a few weeks, waiting for the heat to die down. My food supplies were running low and I made the mistake of calling Ralph to meet me at a designated spot on the back road to Armidale. Ralph came with Charlie Marr, a first cousin and Martin Wombat, young boys about 19 years old, riding their motorbikes. The boys had money so I sent them up to Armidale to buy food. I wasn't keen to go with the boys but they persuaded me, dropping me off about 15 kilometres short of Armidale. I made myself comfortable with a campfire and waited. Later that night, Charlie and Martin returned in a stolen red Monaro. They had bought food and left their bikes at a cousin's place. Martin had hot-wired the Monaro and during the night the boys had robbed a camping store. I remonstrated with them, "You fools, what were you thinking? You'll bring the heat back on me. We've got to get going. The place will be swarming with cops soon."

We drove back down the Armidale Road. Stopping near Lower Creek, I lifted up part of a fence, wire and posts while the boys drove the car under and hid it in the bush. The gate still had an untampered padlock on it so if the police checked they wouldn't think anyone had gone through. With both the car and ourselves hidden under the scrub we waited.

Sure enough, within hours police cars were driving up and down the Armidale Road and the next day a helicopter flew overhead.

I complained to Ralph, "You shouldn't have bought anyone with you." I thought, "Those young boys have no sense, you can't depend on them to be still or quiet enough."

I crawled away from them and hid in a log. Six times the helicopter flew over but no-one saw me. When it was safe to attempt a trip to the cave I had no intention of taking young Charlie or Martin with me. I realised I had to get those boys out of there or I would surely be caught.

In the dark the boys drove the car back to the road. I made Martin drive while I sat in the passenger seat ready to jump out at the first sign of trouble. Soon we came close to Bellbrook. I knew the cops would be thick in the little town so I stopped the car to take out the rear light bulbs. It was one o'clock in the morning when we approached the long, long hill that led into the small, historic town of Bellbrook. About a kilometre before town I took the wheel, cut the engine and switched off the headlights. Noiselessly the car rolled right through the town. Although we passed about thirty police cars, a helicopter idle and unguarded and tracker dogs straining at their leashes, barking from the back of a paddy wagon, no-one stirred. We drove on through the outskirts of Kempsey via Sherwood and all the way to Taree, dropping Ralph off at Port Macquarie along the way. The following day the search continued from Bellbrook but I was miles away.

The page 2 of the Saturday edition of the Macleay Argus November 19, 1988 an article by the reporter Vanessa Kennedy carried a poor photograph of my face with the caption. **'Have you seen this man?'**

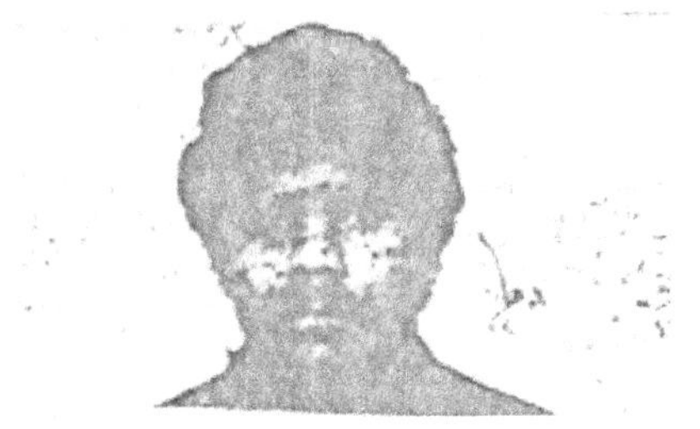

If you have seen this man contact the nearest police station immediately.

Police have commended the public on their assistance during the search for three fugitives but ask people to ensure their information is clear and accurate. Search Commanding officer, Detective Bon Williams said not all reorted sightings have been correct leaving police concentrating on the wrong area.

He said it is only through the help of the public that tabs have been kept on the men. He said the men must have to stop for fuel, food and to sleep so people should be on the alert. Anyone with information would call their nearest police station immediately.

This was immediately followed by:

Rambo still fugitive still on the loose

Police believe a Rambo style fugitive who has been on the loose in the Macleay, Hastings and New England districts is now on his way to Sydney.

The 26-year-old former Bellbrook man may be dressed in camouflage and is believed to be armed with rifled, and machetes stolen from an Armidale disposal store early Thursday morning. Two accomplices have joined him - one is believed to be his 20 year old brother. The men have been evading police since escaping in a high powered car chase around the streets of Kempsey on Tuesday afternoon.

Sear commanding officer, Detective Sergeant Bob Wiliiona said both air and ground searches were conducted on Thursday in the Belllbrook and Armidale areas. He said the fugitives are armed and dangerous. He said some of the Aboriginal community are fearing for their lives.

The men were last sighted early yesterday heading towards Newcastle in a stolen red Holden Monaro. It is believed they are making their way to Sydney.

Sgt Williams said the drama began on Tuesday afternoon in Port Macquarie when police went to a home in Douglas Street to question a 26-year-old Aboriginal man wanted on several charges. He became frightened, smashed through a back window and ran into the bush carrying a rifle. Minutes later he was sighted at the West Port Primary School and it was feared he would take hostages.

Police reinforcements from Kempsey were called but police turned around when a stolen Mazda station wagon was reported racing north on the Pacific Highway. It was spotted in Kempsey at 4:30pm and a wild car chase through the Central Business District ensued. The fugitive escaped police through traffic in West Kempsey's River Street.

Sgt Williams said police began to rely heavily on the public to track the man's next movements.

Sighting were made of him in Bellbrook and later Armidale and the search headed west. One sighting by late Tuesday afternoon had the man, in the company of his brother, heading back to Bellbrook. On Wednesday morning the stolen Mazda was found abandoned in Macksville.

"The public was marvellous providing us with information on his movements but unfortunately some of it was incorrect," Sgt William said. "While we were back in Kempsey investigating a sighting the stolen vehicle turned up in Macksville."

By 5:30am Thursday police had a confirmed sighting of the the men, this time joined by a third Aboriginal. They were seen speeding off in a stolen red Holden Monaro from a n army disposal goods store. The shop had been broken into and a quantity of army camouflage equipment, camping gear and machetes were missing.

The car was later spotted driving into Lower Creek, west of Bellbrook.

Aeroplanes from Kempsey and Armidale airports joined in the search and worked with police ground patrols in the Upper Macleay.

Residents say most of the activity centred around the Bellbrook Aboriginal mission area, where it is believed the men are given assistance. However by early yesterday morning the men had been sighted heading sough. The search in the Upper Macleay area was scaled down and all southern police stations placed on alert.

This article recorded sightings of me near Bellbrook and Armidale. Police assumed my brother, Ralph, was with me in the wild chase through Kempsey but he only joined me later in the day. It was true that some would help the police but most of my aboriginal family and friends gave confusing statements so the police often were looking in the wrong place. It was amazing despite such a huge effort on the part of the police, with cars, a helicopter and tracker dogs that we were able to slip through the net. My ability to outwit the police as much as anything made me such a wanted men. I revelled in outfoxing them and loved the '*Rambo*' label often wearing military style pants and a knife in my belt.

3

CAVEMAN

Like my ancestors before me I felt at home in the cave. I remember those days as some of the most enjoyable of my life. True, I wasn't really free, I was a criminal on the run but I felt free in the cave. I lived much as my forebears did. A nearby spring provided water and I fished the nearby creek for perch. Although I had hooks and lines I should spear fish like my forebears. I knew the hiding places of turtles in the creek. Wallaby, possum and bird were cooked over an open fire. I had camping equipment and tinned food but I could live without them if I had to. In the cool evenings I felt the presence of my ancestors singing, dancing and telling stories around the campfire. I was never lonely there. I remembered the old people - my grandfather, Auntie Man and Bob West. They had told me of a civilisation lost, of good men and bad, corroborees and massacres.

Today it is generally accepted that my people, the Thungutti tribe, occupied a large stretch of land from around Anderson's Sugarloaf to as far south as the Upper Manning. The Macleay River, the main watercourse of their territory, shared a common watershed with two other tributaries, the Manning and Hastings Rivers on the eastern edge of the New England tableland. The tableland is open, undulating country at two to three thousand metres above sea level. From this plateau, the rivers drop about two thousand metres into a maze of ravines, then weave their way through thousands of hectares of heavy forest, deep gorges and mountain ranges finally crossing a narrow coastal plain into the sea. This is knows as Falls Country, so precipitous that it can only be entered on foot or horseback.

The attitude of European invaders to the indigenous inhabitants of Australia was mixed. Some saw them as a gentle people; others as uncivilised savages, conniving and murderous. History records that at the time of the first European contacts with Indigenous Australians they were a happy, healthy and peaceful people. Captain Cook observed that the natives were , 'in no way inclined to cruelty, as appeared from their treatment of one of our people...they appear to some to be the most wretched people on earth, but in reality are far happier that we Europeans....They live in a Tranquility which is not disturbed by the Inequality of Condition,'[1]

Aboriginals did not show much interest in the European's possessions, having no need for them. Cook observed their features were 'far from disagreeable and their voices soft and tuneable.'[2]. Hand-drawn pictures and photographs show the coastal Aborigine as a magnificent specimen, some over six feet tall, well proportioned and athletic in build. They are described as dignified, walking with ease and grace. Even today their athleticism is in evidence, particularly on the football field. The Australian natives were and are a spiritual people. They have a grand accumulation of poetry, songs, dances, dramas, legends and stories.

The original inhabitants were ruled by laws and customs with a minimum of leadership and social caste, a standard modern society would feign imitate. The tribes of the Three Rivers met regularly, and as one people, enjoyed their great festivals, religious, athletic and cultural. Stanner's essays note that 'the Blacks did not fight over land. There were no wars or invasion to seize territory. They did not enslave each other....there is no class division. There is no property or income inequality. The result is homeostasis, far-reaching and stable.'[3]

Aboriginal people fishing, as depicted by French explorers in 1800

Written records of the early settlers and squatters recorded the generosity of the Aborigines, their ready friendship and their happy and contented nature. A few records remain of fights between two tribes, usually to settle an injustice done by an individual of one of the tribes. The opponents would face each other and spears were thrown amid much noise but the instant the fight was concluded, usually by an injury on one side or the other, the two parties would be reconciled and jointly assist attending to the wounded.

Aborigines were well-fed, perhaps better than much of Europe, especially those living in the coastal areas. Hundreds of foods were at their seasonal disposal, more than half of vegetable origin. At the time of European occupation Augustus Rudder, son of an early settler on the Macleay River, Enoch Rudder, wrote that the area was a veritable Garden of Eden, with luxuriant undergrowth, trees of lofty height; the jungle forest literally alive with birds and the water teeming with fish and aquatic birds of many kinds. The Blacks, he said, appeared to be numerous. He recorded watching Aborigines fish in the Macleay from bark canoes, the man with poised spear and often a lubra with a piccaninny at breast tending a small fire on a clay base at the bottom of the craft. [5] Many of these foods disappeared with the introduction of sheep. Cattle stations and sheep runs so depleted their hunting grounds that the danger of starvation became a real possibility.

It is obvious that the Aborigine had no conception of what the arrival of white settlers would do to his way of life. The British government did not regard Australia as 'occupied', therefore its inhabitants had no 'land rights' despite being the only inhabitants for at least four thousand years. Blomfield writes, 'As land hungry settlers moved deeper into Aborigine territory many Aborigines simply gave up and settled on the outskirts of embryo towns and were rapidly corrupted by the evils of Western society or caught European diseases to which they had no inbuilt resistance.....the more spirited of the people retreated into the mountains and gorges of the Falls Country and were joined by people from the New England Tableland, the Hastings and Manning Rivers.'[6]

This remnant turned to spearing cattle and sheep, indeed often driving off hundreds of sheep at a time and murdering shepherds, cedar cutters and on rare occasions, women. In the main the timber cutters were convicts, hardened by the brutality of the times. It appears these men did much to damage relations with the Aborigines, purportedly dispatching the natives with swords fashioned from the blades of their saws. There is only one existing report of Aboriginal murder of white women, when two shepherds and their wives were found murdered on Kunderang Station but many records exist of the murder of Aboriginal men, women and children. The fact that the white men who pursued the offenders are recorded as finding hundreds of Aborigines feasting, with their women and children, shows just how hungry and desperate they had become.

The injury and murders of white people by Aborigines and theft of livestock were written up in the newspapers in graphic detail but massacres of the Aborigines were given little or no mention. The Myall Creek Massacre is of particular note not only because of the barbarity of the murder of at least twenty-seven people but because a white man reported the massacre to the authorities. 'A group of men, consisting of twelve convict settlers and one free man, John Fleming, arrived at a hut on Henry Dangar's Myall Creek Station on 27th June.

They told the station hand there, George Anderson, that they intended to round up any Aboriginal people they could find. They claimed to be acting in retaliation of the theft of cattle, although they did not attempt to identify any individuals who were responsible for the theft. The men gathered up twenty-eight people, mostly women and children, out of a group of forty to fifty Aboriginal people who were camping in the area. They were taken behind a hill, away from the hut. After being raped, tortured, killed and possibly beheaded the bodies were then burnt. When the manager of the station, a Mr. Hobbs, returned several days later and discovered the bodies, he decided to report the incident, travelling 250 miles across the Liverpool Plains to Muswellbrook.'[7]

Eleven convicts were arrested and charged with nine counts of murder. John Fleming, the leader of the massacre, was never captured and was allegedly responsible for further massacres throughout the Liverpool Plains and New England regions.

The jury at the first trial, after deliberating for just twenty minutes, found all eleven men not guilty. One of the jurors later told the newspaper *The Australian* that although he considered the men guilty of murder, he could not convict a white man of killing an aboriginal.[8] "I looked on the blacks as a set of monkeys and the sooner they are exterminated from the face of the earth, the better. I knew the men were guilty of murder but I would never see a white man hanged for killing a black."[4]

A second trial convicted seven of the men who were consequently hanged but the colony as a whole was in an uproar in sympathy for the murderers. Most of the newspapers of the day deplored the hangings while glossing over the original crime. Some like the *Sydney Herald* of October 5th 1838, roundly declared that aboriginals were less than human beings and called, in effect, for their extermination.[8]

Aboriginal resistance from the Falls Country continued for about twenty-five years and provoked retaliation in the form of murder, massacre and mass poisoning. These things are burnt into the race memory of the pitiful remnant of the Thungutti people. Geoffrey Blomfield's book *'Baal Belbora, The End of the Dancing'* documents the horrific tales of murders of aboriginal people, shot, knifed, poisoned, even some thrown over cliffs and one particularly horrendous incident where children's skulls were smashed by stirrups – the deaths of men, women and children by groups of white settlers as a law unto themselves; and without any attempt to apprehend the actual perpetrators of a crime.

In 1788 it was estimated Australia was populated by about 300,000 Aborigines, give or take 50,000 or so. By the time of the white centenary celebrations in 1888 the number was reduced to about 60,000 full bloods.

The Thungutti tribe came from Lower Creek and Kunderang, where some of the most brutal massacres occurred. In the early 1880's this tribe was forced onto a 90 acre settlement at Bellbrook. As the tribes were getting smaller every day the New South Wales government established the Aboriginal Protection Act. The Bellbrook Mission was controlled by the Aboriginal Protection Board. Much later the Seventh-Day Adventist Church became involved. Ten tribal initiated leaders were chosen by the New South Wales government to clear the land. Four of these men were Charlie's great great grandfathers; Ralph Quinlan, Lockey Vale, Wombo Murray and Reynold Holten. The land was deeded to these men by the Queen.

Aboriginal activist, Ray Kelly, documented the effect of mission life. 'Although these missions provided some kind of protection for our people from extinction, it is obvious the missions were used to bring our people under control. Once our people were on these missions it was safe for the white farmers to squat on land that was rightfully ours. When this happened our people were facing depression. They no longer had free access to the hundreds of square miles of tribal land they once proudly roamed.

They were now confined to ninety acres. Because of this the will to be self-supporting was now lost. So the Government introduced rations and hand-outs to our people, again taking away the will to be self-supporting. Of course, there were some people who wanted to break away from this style of life but were afraid to do so because they feared what might happen to them. So they accepted this style of life.

Only certain people were allowed to leave the mission with the manager's approval. No Aboriginal strangers were allowed to camp near these missions. No one was let in or out without a white man's consent. Under these conditions it was impossible for any of us to feel proud of ourselves, and our Aboriginal knowledge quickly began to fade away. The last of the initiations to be performed in our tribe was held in the late 1930's. Many of the old fully initiated men were now dying without passing on the information to the un-initiated men. We were now in a cultural bind.'[8]

My paternal grandfather had organised that last initial and corroboree to take place at Bellbrook; in stages up in the mountains. I had been too young to take part. Hiding in my cave I had plenty of time to consider the history of my tribe and my own experience with white authority.

In many ways I reflected the Aboriginal native. I was tall with a well built physique, I knew how to survive in the bush and to those that knew me I had a easy going, generous and happy attitude to life but I also identified with the hostile remnant, disposed of their traditional lands and prepared to put up a bitter though uneven fight.

I despised white authority which I regarded as prejudiced. They treated my family as criminals even though I was the criminal and did not understand our family values so they felt justified in attacking anyone associated with me verbally and even physically. That just increased my defiance for white authority. On the other hand I treated native authority with respect.

......

1. Geoffrey Blomfield, *Baal Belbora*, 1981 p.8, Alternative Publishing Co-Operative, Sydney, Australia

2. Geoffrey Blomfield, *Baal Belbora*, 1981 p.8, Alternative Publishing Co-Operative, Sydney, Australia

3. W.E.H. Stanner, *Whiteman Got no Dreaming*, Essays 1938-1973 p.27

4. Geoffrey Blomfield, *Baal Belbora*, 1981 p.28, Alternative Publishing Co-Operative, Sydney, Australia

5. 4. Geoffrey Blomfield, *Baal Belbora*, 1981 pp. 22-23, Alternative Publishing Co-Operative, Sydney, Australia

6. http://en.wikeipedia.org/wiki/Myall_Creek-massacre sighted 15.03.09

7. Russell Ward, *'Massacre at Myall Creek', The Good Weekend, Sydney Morning Herald,* 05/11/1977

8. "Myall Creek Massacre", Parliament of New South Wales Hansard, June 8, 2000

9. www.environment.nsw.gov.au/resources/cultureheritage/RevivalRenewalReturnLegacy.pdf Ray Kelly, *From the "Cultural Bind" to a solution: the survey of Aboriginal sacred sites in New South Wales*

4

MY MOTHER'S STORY

I don't remember ever living with my mother. There wasn't a time I can remember my Mum and Dad living together and I never asked why. Dad worked in the bush, fencing, grubbing, ring-barking for white fellas. He'd only be home once a month, sometimes for a week-end, so I was mostly raised by my aunties. Dad's two sisters and their husbands lived on the Reserve and they helped Dad out. I had an older brother Billy and a younger sister Jenny.

Billy was taken when I was small. I was told about it but I don't remember the time he was taken away. He went to foster homes then Kitchener Boys Home but when he was eighteen he came up to Bellbrook Reserve looking for me. Jenny was living with Mum but she was taken and put into Cootamundra Girls Home. I was the only one that escaped. I thank God for that but we never lived as a proper family; that was stolen from us.

Life was tough on Bellbrook Reserve. Our home was a shack, part weatherboard, part tin, just two big rooms and an old hessian sack for a door. In winter Dad's sister would sew sacks together to make blankets for me. There was no electricity, gas or hot water so one of my jobs was to cut and fetch wood every afternoon after school. We cooked on a wood stove and washed clothes in the creek, hanging the clothes out on rocks. We could bathe in a copper but mostly the other kids and I would bathe in the creek. In winter the pipes froze and I'd have to cart water from the creek for cooking and drinking.

In those days no-one had a car, but there were lots of horses on the reserve. Dad would ride to work. We kids would ride on horseback or jump the creek or if we had any money we'd catch a bus to Bellbrook to go to the picture theatre. Mostly we would walk barefoot as we didn't have shoes.

One good thing about the Reserve was our school. The building is still standing today although not used as a school now. We had lots of students there. Mr. Bates was the teacher and the manager of the Reserve as well. He and his wife had a nice house on the Reserve. I loved going to school. When I was fifteen Mr. Bates said to me, "There's no need for you to come to school tomorrow, go to my home and my wife will show you what to do." I went to the toilets and cried and cried but there was nothing I could do; we had no choice in those days. If you complained they said you would be taken away and put in a girl's home or a foster home so we just did what we were told.

So the next day I went to Mrs. Bates' place to clean and cook for her, five days a week. At the end of the week I got a small box of rations – half a pound of tea, half a pound of butter, a small packet of white flour and a small packet of white sugar. Yes, life was hard. After work I still had jobs to do at home; chop and bag wood, cook damper and wash the clothes in the creek.

Once a week the manager's wife or a welfare worker would go into all the homes, check the kids for nits and see if the sheets were clean. If they weren't satisfied they'd take the kids away. We lived in fear but my aunties; they always kept our place clean. I was little lighter coloured than most of the other children on the Reserve and all my childhood I was scared of being taken from my family.

There was a big church building on the Reserve, a Seventh-Day Adventist Church. We were pretty much all Adventists at Bellbrook Reserve, though some not practising. My Dad was big on religion. He would go door to door reading the Bible with people, just like a minister. People say I take after Dad. Religion was a big part of our lives. We didn't drink, or smoke or take drugs like some young people do today.

One of my friends all through school was Ralph Quinlan. We got close but our parents didn't approve so my Auntie sent me away with a friend, Dorothy Caldwell. Dorothy and I boarded the train at Kempsey but after the train pulled out of the station what a surprise! There was Ralph on the train. He didn't tell me before but he'd come to the station and hidden in the long grass. Kempsey Station was just in a paddock in those days and as the train started moving he jumped on. For a while we lived at Mungindi on the Queensland border. Ralph and I lived together at first then we were married proper on the Bellbrook Reserve. I was twenty-two then and Ralph a couple of years older.

Ralph and I had eight children and Charlie was the eldest, named after my Dad, Charles Louis Holten. He was named Charles Frederick Quinlan but we called him Charlie or Fred. Charlie was granddad's favourite and he spoiled him. Charlie was born in Kempsey hospital on the 29th September 1962. At that time we lived in Greenhills on the outskirts of Kempsey with Ralph's mum while Ralph worked away on the railways. When Charlie was 12 we bought a railway house at Kundabung.

Ralph was a workaholic. He worked every day but Saturday. Each Sunday he'd have us all out working, even the children. We'd pick beans or peas or dig potatoes. We all hated it but Ralph was strict; you never said no.

One day we'd been picking beans at Kinchela near South West Rocks and we'd come back to a cousin's house for lunch. Ralph had a shower and was having a lie down because he was feeling sick but he hadn't told anyone. He was sitting on the bottom stairs reading his Bible and called out to me for a drink of water. I went upstairs to get him the water and when I came down he was lying on the ground gasping for air. I asked him what was the matter but he couldn't answer - he was having a massive heart attack. Ralph was only young, only 32.

My screams bought all the adults and children around. Charlie, being the eldest, cradled his dad's head in his arms and Ralph died right there. Someone went for an ambulance but it took ages to come. The ambulance men took Ralph to Kempsey Hospital but he was already dead. I was crying and all the kids were crying too. The little ones knew something was wrong but they didn't know what. Charlie understood what had happened and he was devastated.

I was in shock because it was so sudden. Overnight I was left with eight children and no support. My Dad had died a bit earlier. I was at a camp meeting when the hospital called about Dad. Dad wasn't expected to last the night but he was talking fine when I saw him. He asked me to go to Kundabung and get his mail with his pay check. I never spoke to him again. When I got back the sister came to me and said he'd passed away. She held me, didn't want me to go up to the room but I pushed her away and went up and held my dad and I cried and cried. I thought it was the end of the world when he died; he had always been there for me. I had two good men in my life and now they were both dead.

Ralph's funeral was one of the biggest in the district. His friend, Andrew Pacy, a white fella wrote a piece that was printed in the Macleay Argus June12, 1975. This is what he had to say under the title: ***"A man says goodbye to a friend".***

> *"Sir: I have just returned from the funeral of Ralph Quinlan, who was employed by the railways at Kundabung.*
>
> *Mr Quinlan was an Aborigine and I knew him very well. He was raised at Bellbrook, being the son of Mr. and Mrs. Joe Quinlan. He was a man held in great respect by his people and by the whites. Because of that, I must say it was one of the biggest funerals I have attended.*
>
> *Pastor Rosenthal and Pastor Thomas, of the Seventh Day Adventist church, officiated at the church and the graveside and the service they conducted was really touching. The hymns they sang had to be heard to be described. I can only say it was all beautiful.*

Apart from all this we couldn't help noticing the entrance to the cemetery where railwaymen formed a guard of honour. These men were white and they went to the trouble of doing this for one Aborigine and that really deserves mention in my book.

Mr. Quinlan, as I knew him, was a hard-working man who died suddenly at the young age of 32 on Monday June 2. He was with his wife who was doing charitable work at the time. She is a tireless worker among our people and is left with eight children, the eldest being 12 and the youngest one. I have known this family for a long time. They came to love the Word at an early age.

My deepest sympathy goes out to Mrs. Quinlan and her family and I am sure most people will join me in saying: God be with you."

After Ralph died, friends helped us out. We lived with Esther and George Quinlan for while before going back to Bellbrook Reserve. It was here I made a really big mistake, one I regret to this day. We had a new pastor, Pastor Thompson. He'd come from New Guinea and I don't know if that was why but I thought he was a hard man. He went through the church roll to see who was coming to church and struck folk off the roll. I was very committed to Jesus, teaching Sabbath School, visiting neighbours trying to bring them to the Lord.

I had started spending time with an old friend from school. We'd been sweet on each other back then. Soon tongues started wagging but we weren't doing anything wrong. Pastor Thompson and Pastor George called a church meeting and I was censored for three months. At the meeting Auntie May Mosley stood up for me. She quoted scripture to those pastors, 'He that is without sin among you, let him cast a stone at her,' and everyone went really quiet.

Pastor Thompson told her to sit down, it wasn't her business. So they censored me.

Auntie May took me home to comfort me but I could not be comforted. I was young, falsely accused and I knew others in the church were really sinning and nothing was done about it so I left the church; for ten years I left the church. I think back now and wonder why I did that; I regret, I regret.

Charlie, loosing first his grandfather then his father as well as my leaving the church affected him a great deal. When Ralph was alive the family worshipped morning and evening, church every Sabbath. The boys dressed in suits and neckties and the girls in dresses singing choruses all the way the church. Now Charlie started to go his own way, getting into the wrong crowd. Charlie was close to his younger brother Ralph and the two of them started to get into trouble. I regret.

5

CHILDHOOD

My earliest memory of my childhood was walking along the river banks with my grandfather, Charlie Holten. I was named after my maternal grandfather and the old man had a particular liking for me. As in days long gone he felt it a duty to educate me about my Aboriginal heritage and ties with the Thunguntti land. On weekends and for weeks at a time during school holidays I would camp with my grandfather in the bush around the Lower Creek area,

While grandpa was grubbing lantana around the river banks, felling trees or fencing, I would pass the tools, unconsciously soaking up knowledge that would become a permanent part of my being. In the evenings grandfather would relate stories about life when he was growing up before before the Bellbrook reserve existed. That was the time when the Thungutti people still roamed they ancestral lands, although becoming more and more restricted by the pastoral holdings of the 'invaders'. Grandpa worked for the pastoralists now but he took the time to instil in me a pride for my tribe and its heritage.

Each tribe had its own token. The Thungutti's token was a praying mantis. Grandpa would tell me stories about the praying mantis and then he would whistle a special tune. Praying mantises would come out of their hiding places amongst the leaves and dance, swaying back and forth to the sound of the song. Grandpa would reminisce about the days Lenny Ducat, my great Uncle would dance the praying mantis dance and sing at special tribal ceremonies. How I loved my grandpa. He made me proud to be a Thungutti man.

From him I leant the skills that enabled me to survive alone in the bush. He taught me to spear fish. Perch, mullet and pink-eye were plentiful in the Five-day creek. We cooked turtle whole on coals. I could spear a kangaroo, bleed it and skin in. Overnight the carcass would hang from a tree and the next day we would butcher it, eating everything but the guts. Nothing was wasted in the primitive life and no life taken unnecessarily. Grandpa would make damper and fish stew, sometimes soup with potato or pumpkin.

From grandfather and Auntie Mun, another Thungutti elder, I learnt some Thungutti language. Thungutti was not a written language and I couldn't speak it well but I could understand the elders when they spoke and to this day I remember a lot of language. Thungutti is also spelt 'Dhungutti'. The 'th' which used to be rolled in speech becoming the easier to pronounce 'd' sound. Sadly, today many Indigenous people do not know the correct pronunciation of their tribal language. Aboriginal elders had their Aboriginal names as well as English names. Later I would be called 'Oker' meaning Aboriginal hit-man.

On the reserve it was forbidden to speak Thungutti, a mindless, senseless restriction that resulted in the loss of many tribal words. The survival of the Thungutti language can be attributed a dedicated group of people who wrote a dictionary, phonetically English, to preserve what has been remembered of that ancient communication. Yes, I was proud of my heritage and of my family. I understood that I came from a 'royal family'; my blood line exclusively the Vale, Quinlan, Holten, Murray and Calligan families. These families had intermarried preserving the Thungutti blood. As the oldest son I inherited responsibility as a future leader in the tribe.

As a young boy I played with other boys at the Reserve but perhaps because of the time spent with my grandfather and perhaps isolation due to a bout of rheumatic fever, or due to the strict upbringing of my deeply religious family I was a loner. At first I didn't get into trouble with the other boys because I kept to himself.

The death of my grandfather and shortly later my father's death devastated me. My mother leaving the church and busy raising eight children combined to make my secure world fall apart. Still the early influences of my hardworking grandparents and parents should have been sufficient to keep me on the right track but for one thing, I had become a fighter. I, the loner, desired the respect and envy of my peers so I did what came naturally to me as a strapping and fearless lad; I became a brawler.

It started at school. I was expelled from Port Macquarie High, Wauchope High and Kempsey High for fighting. I applied the same strategy in playing footy; tackle hard, pile drive the opponent into the ground then use my elbow. At the end of the season if there had been a prize for the player most sent off during a game I would have won it without opposition.

"Come on Charlie, there's a fight fixed for you tonight," a school mate would whisper through the window.

I should have been at church on Friday night but instead I was sneaking out at night for a fight. Sixty or more boys and girls would form a ring at the show ground, on a Port beach or behind a school building. The champion of each gang of boys would face up, take off their shirts and fight with bare knuckles until one was knocked out or gave up, bloodied and beaten. Bets were made on the outcome. I was considered the best fighter in Wauchope and Port Macquarie.

One night word came that a bloke from Sydney was up who reckoned he could wallop me. The fight lasted about fifteen seconds. The boys dragged the braggart onto the road while one of the girls called an ambulance then everyone fled. My opponent never squealed; it was a matter of honour.

Even though I liked to fight my strict religious upbringing had instilled in me some sense of right and wrong. During the time I attended Kempsey High School, I and two mates were walking back to Greenhill after footy practice. My mates decided to steal some corn from a crop behind Turner's take-away shop. I wouldn't join them, saying I wasn't allowed to steal. Instead I sat on the curb opposite Turner's shop.

A short while later a police car drove up and the policemen grabbed me. They wanted to know where the other boys were but I wouldn't talk. When the police headed for Turner's shop, the boys came out with their hands in the air crying, "Don't shoot, don't shoot."

All three of us were taken to the police station and charged with breaking and entering. Each boy was made to empty his pockets. The other two boys took out lollies and other food but all I had on me was my handkerchief and a hairbrush. My silence, because I wouldn't tell on a mate, resulted in me being charged with the others, although I was completely innocent and did not even know the if boys had entered the shop. That injustice made an impact on me. I was starting to reason if I'm accused unfairly why not actually do the crime.

I was proud of my prowess with my fists, I was angry of the deaths of my loved ones, I resented the authoritarian attitude on the Bellbrook Reserve and I was upset about the way my tribe had been treated in the past. The fuse was lit for trouble but I was unaware of the direction my life was about to suddenly take.

6

LIVING WITH WHITE FOLKS

While still in school I became a ward of the Mackay family. The Mackay family were white folk but were work friends of my dad and also attended church which was always super important to my dad. Gretchen Elva MacKay's attitude to people reflected her upbringing. Her father left the family for England before she was born leaving her mother to raise her and older brother Fred. An old photo of her father showed Gretchen had inherited his fair curly hair while Fred had the dark straight hair of his mother. Perhaps that was the reason Fred was the 'pet' of the family with 'wretched' Gretchen the uncared-for 'slave'. Gretchen was first out of bed, straight to the wood heap to split chips and cut wood for the old combustion stove. The big strawberry patch needed weeding and there were always vegetables to plant and washing to do. The slightest infringement led to a strapping.

Even though her mother was a dressmaker, Gretchen was clothed in rags; a barefoot student at the local school when she was allowed to attend. Worse was to come when her mother married the 'lolly man'. Lollies were replaced by drunken beatings by Les while under the influence of alcohol. Even Gretchen's mother was bashed senseless. Gretchen's memories were dominated by fear and worthlessness. Even her little friends, two lovely Persian kittens were tied in a bag by her stepfather and before her eyes thrown to their deaths from the swing bridge at the Botanical Gardens. Gretchen was too terrified to reveal the problems at home until at the age of fourteen she found the courage to run away.

As soon as she was able Gretchen discarded her first name and used her second name, Elva. As she grew up away from her home, kind people healed the pain to a degree and now married with three children she was determined to show her own children the love and affection that she had never experienced as a child. At different times her home became a home away from home for any child, or even an animal in need.

Elva and her husband John were Christians. Every Friday night they would sing around the piano. Two out of four Friday nights a knock would be heard at the door. I would be there with my big, beaming, unforgettable smile that would melt Elva's heart. I rode the train from Kempsey to Wauchope to get to the MacKay's home. I mostly was barefoot and wore dirty clothes but the Mackay family loved me. Their sons, Calvyn and Rodney, knew me from school and sometimes I would stay the whole weekend.

Elva used to play piano for the Wauchope Church as well as running the children's Sabbath School. Occasionally my mother would bring some of her girls. My mum had also visited the Mackay home a few times with two little girls and a baby in tow. Some months after the death of Ralph, she came with pleading eyes to the front door.

"Elva, would you take Charlie and look after him?"

I was becoming a handful and mum was desperate for help. How could Elva say no? She had been a child once and someone took her in. So at the age of twelve I became a part of the Mackay family. The welfare would come from time to time to see how I as getting on. My life fell apart after my dad died and I felt okay about the arrangement as Mum wasn't coping and really it was common in our culture for aunts and uncles, even just friends, to help look after children from time to time.

John Mackay had a partnership in a timber business, the Pamelva Timber Company, named after Pam and Elva, the men's wives. While his partner worked in the sawmill John cut timber in the bush. Elva ran a florist business from home, but on hot days the closed sign would go up as soon as the children came home from school. Elva would take Calvin, Rodney, me and their youngest, a daughter Brenda out into the bush where John was working. The family would share a large, cold watermelon. Then the fight was on; two teams lined up hurling broken bits of watermelon skin at each other.

I loved the trips to the bush and enjoyed working in the sawmill. All the boys had opportunity to earn a few dollars sweeping the floor, stacking timbers, even using the saws as they got older. I have good memories of my years with the MacKay family. They treated me fairly like one of their own. Whenever one of Elva's children was bought a new shirt, a fishing rod or a bicycle I got one too. The many white Australian friends my father had and the influence of the MacKay family enabled me to feel comfortable around white folk.

At that time I was a well-mannered boy who kept my room spotless, helped with the dishes and did not cause any trouble. Sometimes a police car would follow me home or stop down the road from the house as if they were just waiting for me to do something wrong. The police were after the dark boys looking for an excuse to lock them up and that bothered Elva. Truth be known her own sons were more likely to get into trouble. Some of their mates from high school were not the best examples. Boys tended to turn up at the MacKay place for toasted sandwiches and bike riding and Elva encouraged them to come to her home where she could keep an eyes on things. Once she found some marijuana plants growing on the roof and suspected that things could be going on behind her back.

We amused ourselves with the usual boyhood pranks, hanging around the golf course looking for balls, collecting bird's eggs and stealing the milk money from the neighbouring houses and blowing up mailboxes with firecrackers. One of our favourite tricks was to phone the school principal.

"Is Mr. Wall there?"

"No," he would answer, "there's no Mr. Wall here."

"Well is Mrs. Wall there?"

"No, there's no Mrs. Wall here," the principal would reply.

"Well what's holding up your roof then," Rodney would say laughing hysterically.

He always caught him out.

Even though Calvyn was the same age as me, Rodney, a year younger, was my best friend. Calvyn had a different nature to the easy going Rodney, a nasty streak and was more selfish. Rodney explains Calvyn's temperament as being due to the disease haemochromatosis. Both boys inherited the defective gene from their parents. Haemochromatosis is named the 'silent killer' because most people are unaware they have it. It causes extra iron to gradually build up in the body's tissues and organs, a term called iron overload. If the iron build-up is untreated, it can, over many years, damage the body's organs.

Rodney found out he had haemochromatosis when he was sick with Ross River Fever but Calvyn had never been treated. Perhaps this explains Calvyn's bitterness after the motorcycle accident. It was a Sunday morning and we were riding motorcycles in a friend's paddock. Calvyn had stopped his bike at the bottom of a hill but I, being as I thought an experienced rider, came flying down the hill and ran straight into Calvyn. One of Calvyn's hands smashed into front headlight, cutting it severely. The wound required microsurgery. He never let me forget the accident.

Elva's husband, John, had been a boxer. At the age of eighteen he had been a champion middleweight, winning twenty fights out of twenty-two bouts. Elva did not approve but John taught us boys to box. We would watch the boxing on television with John but Elva could not stand to watch the fights as they reminded her of her childhood beatings.

The boys and I had the odd blue but all the boys did a bit of fighting around Wauchope. Rodney never wanted to fight but his brother arranged the fights and he couldn't back out. I did more fighting than the other boys. Once a fight started the strategy was cause maximum damage as soon as possible. Calvyn and Rodney experimented with drugs but I never did. My dad's religion was strongly opposed to any type of drug, including alcohol. It's probably the reason I'm still alive today.

My friendship with Rodney continued even after I left the MacKay's. Although Rodney knew I was on the run from the police, he was unaware of the extent of my crimes and could not bring himself to dob me in. One time I rang Rodney to ask him to take me up to Stanthorpe to visit John, Rodney's dad. Rodney agreed so he, myself and my girl-friend drove up in Rodney's escort panel van. About ten kilometres before Walcha a highway patrol car went past. "If that car turns around, stop and let me out," I said. The police car did turn around so Rodney stopped and I leapt out and disappeared over a hill. The police questioned Rodney, "Who got out of the car?"

"Just a hitchhiker we picked up," Rodney lied.

The police left. There didn't seem any real reason they had turned to follow us.

After driving a few kilometres up the road and checking there were no police in sight Rodney drove back and tried to find me. He hung around for hours as it was a freezing cold day and I wasn't wearing warm clothes. I did not appear so Rodney eventually gave up and drove into Walcha. Rodney knew that I always carried guns for shooting game so he searched the car and found I'd left behind a 38 Special. Quickly he drove out of town and dumped the gun.

Back in Walcha he waited in front of the pub. Once again police surrounded the van and this time searching it. In the end I didn't turn up so they drove on to Rodney's dad's place at Stanthorpe. I had spent those hours walking overland to an Aboriginal settlement at Armidale. The creeks were freezing cold so I crossed them unclothed, then dressed again, keeping warm by being constantly on the more.

Another time Rodney's friendship with me landed him in more serious trouble. Rodney and his heavily pregnant partner, Rose, were living in Port Macquarie. Two of my sisters turned up. "Can we leave this car with you?" they asked, "It's Charlie's."

"It's not hot is it?" Rodney wanted to know.

They assured him it was not stolen. It was early in the morning; the girls pushed the keys into his hand and Rodney went back to the flat not even looking at the car. He and Rose did not have a vehicle at the time so Rose suggested Rodney ring my mum to see if they could use the car to go shopping. He could hear me whispering to my mother in the background,

"Sure, just get the stuff out of the back seat."

Rodney went out to the vehicle; a Falcon, and moved it to the front of his flat. He thought to himself; there was only a blanket on the back seat so he checked the boot; nothing there. Deciding to take out the blanket Rodney grabbed it and felt the gun butts.

"You mongrel," he thought.

He didn't want any heat around his place. His unfriendly neighbour knew he smoked the odd joint and had not approved of me visiting. Rodney felt sure she would dob him in at the first opportunity.

While he was thinking whether to hide the guns in his house or just lock up the car he felt a tap, tap on his shoulder. He turned round to face four coppers.

"What have you got there?" one of them asked. "Looks like guns to me."

The police tried to make Rodney pick up a gun but Rodney knew his fingerprints were not on those guns so he refused. Next they searched Rodney's flat and found two ounces of cannabis. As a consequence Rodney got charged for possession of firearms and drugs. In court the police claimed they had found Rodney carrying the firearms in his front yard and he got six months. On appeal Rodney was found not guilty but the incident is still on his record.

A week or so after that I was back in town and got shot by police at the back of my mother's house. Being my friend was a dangerous business. I would use those whom I trusted not to dob me in. That day the guns were not meant to be in the car. I couldn't park the car at his mothers' place or the police would know I was there so I asked my sister to park the car at Rodney's place. I never meant to put others in trouble but that is often what happened. Did I really care? I was too busy looking after my only skin to give others a second's thought.

7

———

ANGRY YOUNG MAN

I left the MacKay's when I was about fifteen years old, travelling back and forth from Bellbrook to Sydney taking on odd jobs. Although I was a street fighter as yet I had never been in serious trouble with the law. I remember my age clearly; seventeen years and eight months. I was walking down the main street of Kempsey when I saw about eight policemen beating a white man, hitting him with batons. Without thinking I ran across the road.

"What's going on?" I said to one of the policemen.

The policeman's response was to hit me with a baton and I just responded automatically swinging with my fists. Hearing the ruckus some other dark fellas came out of the nearby pub and joined in the fight. The whole affair turned into a nasty brawl.

I vividly remember my feelings about that fight. Flashing through my mind came images of my dead father and grandfather and the massacres at Kunderang. I had wondered whether those stories about the massacres were really true but seeing the police brutality that day convinced me of their validity. My bottled-up emotions and anger were released and I simply went berserk. I threw one *gandhibal* through the pub window, knocked another to the ground and jumped on him trying to break his neck, broke the arm of another and the leg of another. In all eight policeman wound up in hospital. Meanwhile reinforcements had been called in and eventually a mass of officers subdued the white man, the four Aboriginal men and me.

The six of us were taken to the Kempsey lock-up where we were bashed with batons, fingerprinted and put in a cell overnight. The oldest Koori bloke was about thirty years old, the youngest about twenty-five. Next day in court the oldest one was sentenced to six months, the youngest got two months, another one month and the white man was fined and released.

Speaking to me, the judge said, "Mister Quinlan, there is no room in society for a bloke like you. I don't feel any remorse for sentencing you to one and a half years in Grafton Prison."

I was angry. I felt I had done the honourable thing in protecting a victim as I saw it, and here I was sentenced to a prison for difficult offenders, the dumping ground for uncontrollable inmates from other prisons and hard core criminals. The other four who received lighter sentences were sent to the Maitland Jail.

Handcuffed, I was transported to Grafton in the company of an older man, perhaps fifty years old. His name was Tex Reed. He was being transferred to Grafton Jail because he had been in trouble at his previous internment, Bathurst Jail.

"It's a dangerous place, Grafton Jail, young fella," he said, "What yer in fer?

"One and a half years for bashing coppers."

"Well, you'll be in for a shock at Grafton. Listen to me and I'll tell yer what to do."

"No-one's going to put one over me, I'm my own boss," I replied, punching the side of the wagon, "I'll fight anyone and I don't care."

"You got to change your attitude, sonny. They won't mess around with you up there," the old man warned. "Yer only young. Why'd didn't they send yer to Maitland?"

"They said it was because I was the worst. Don't worry old man; no-one will touch you around me."

Tex threw his head back and laughed, "Look, listen to me and you'll get through yer time. They'll bash yer up here."

"No-one's going to bash me," I bragged.

As we were marched through the gates of Grafton Jail, he gave me a last warning, "Put yer hands on yer head."

I ignored him.

Past the next door, the 'welcoming party' were waiting. The party consisted of eight screws armed with batons. They started whaling in on me and the old man. I tried to protect Tex but it was hard to take a swing with my hands in handcuffs. The batons were made out of plaited lead so bruises formed on the inside but didn't show on the outside. The number of warders increased and we were beaten on our arms, legs, all over our bodies until I felt numb, lying on the ground visibly shaking.

I could hardly walk but they made me get up, take off all my clothes and walk through another set of gates into a sort of holding yard, above the warders who were standing around on a grated walkway, looking down on us. Another lot were waiting for us, another beating. This time I didn't hit back; I was too sore. As quickly as it had begun the beating stopped and we were left alone for about ten minutes before hoses were brought in and the blood was hosed off. I watched the red stream drain down a hole in the middle of the yard. Shivering and cold, we waited again. It was now night time.

Tex and I were dressed in the green prison uniform of Grafton Jail; my number 2460 in bold black letters, high on the left hand side of my green shirt. Warders marched us to our cell. Ours was a small, square-shaped room with two fold-down beds on opposite walls. Every detail was indelibly marked on my brain. Cement floor painted burgundy, walls made of cream cement and a tin bucket for the toilet. Apart from the uniform and a pair of black shoes, my possessions consisted of one comb, one toothbrush, a tube of toothpaste, a towel, aluminium cup, plate and spoon. The older man was still giving me advice.

"Make sure yer bed's made in the morning, put your polished shoes in front of the door and clean yer fingernails or they'll bash yer."

I was all in and could only manage a meek, "Yea, yea," in reply.

The next morning the bell sounded once.

"Quickly get up," the old man ordered and started instructing me how to fold the sheets and place the blanket at the foot of the bed.

We could hear the warders coming as we rushed to complete the tasks. By the time the door opened, Tex and I were standing facing the wall, our noses an inch off burgundy.

"What's your number?" a warden demanded.

"I don't know!" I was belligerent.

Slam, my face hit the wall.

"What's your number?"

"Twenty-four sixty."

Slam my face hit the wall again.

I started to remonstrate, "What do you think ...."

Smash, I was hit with a baton.

"I didn't ask you to talk. New guy eh, always gives us trouble in the beginning," the warder smirked as he delivered another blow. "Whose shoe is this?" the same man demanded.

This time I didn't answer and was giving a beating for not answering!

So it went on day after day. I learnt the slightest misdemeanour would result in a beating and sometimes I would be beaten just because the guards felt like it. In the end I learnt to accept the beatings; sometimes fighting back, sometimes just taking it.

"You're going to beat me up anyway," I would say, "so go ahead."

The screws expected to walk in and see their faces reflected from the floor so I kept my cell shiny and clean until eventually the guards developed a grudging respect for me. I was getting tough on the outside but inside I was getting angrier and angrier.

A typical prison day started with inspection at first bell then we were marched out to a breakfast consisting a big spoonful of porridge with no sugar, a piece of toast and a hot drink. I did not drink tea or coffee so I was given a mug of hot water. Back in the cell Tex chucked his porridge onto the wall where it stuck fast! Before eating I would have to pick out the cockroaches and weevils in my food.

After breakfast I joined the chain gang, smashing rocks. After a couple of sandwiches and a piece of fruit for lunch it was back to the rocks, dinner then bed. No T.V, no wireless. I was permitted to write a letter once a month but I never did. I was allowed a visitor once a month but never had one. My mother was too busy looking after my brothers and sisters on her own and I did not expect a visit. I felt that I'd got myself into trouble and I did not want to disgrace the family. I was still the loner, just as I had been in my childhood and youth.

In prison Tex took the place of my estranged family. I always preferred the company of older men and Tex was an interesting old man. His passion was trapping foxes. On the outside he collected bounty money for each fox and sold the pelts. Years later we served time together at Glen Innes Prison. There was a lot of freedom at that institution, no walls. Tex used to work on the farm's pine plantation and I worked in the sawmill. As fox hunting season drew near Tex would start getting excited. He'd save up his tea-bags and sugar. Tex was an avid tea-drinker, he'd even smoke the leaves. Myself and other prisoners would contribute to his haul.

At the opening of the fox hunting season Tex would 'escape'; actually just work away from the pine forest and that's the last the authorities would see of him for the season. The first the officers knew that Tex missing was at the afternoon roll call. The prisoners were required to stand on small squares for the roll but when Tex's number was called, the first day of the hunting season, he would be absent. He would be holed up in the bush trapping foxes. At the end of the season someone would spot him in town or at a park and he'd be re-arrested. Eventually the officers wised-up and wouldn't let Tex on the farm during fox-hunting season. I learnt a lot from Tex's stories of the cunning foxes. A fox would face his pursuers then circle round and follow them. The hunted became the hunter. Later, on the run, I would use this tactic to outwit the police. Tex was a thin man and felt the cold so I gave him my prisoner-issue big army coat. The fact that Tex was a white man made no difference to me; I always liked to look after the old people.

My time in Grafton Penitentiary was not memorable except for a couple of occasions. Once I was bitten by a snake while cutting bush in a swamp. We were all waist up in the swamp when the snake struck. My hip swelled up and I spent a few days in sick bay under the supervision of 'Doctor Death'. A lot of men died in sick bay under Doctor Death's treatment.

The other incident of note occurred when I was getting the regulatory haircut. No-one was allowed a razor blade so shaves and haircuts were done by the prison 'barber'. Nor could a prisoner grow a moustache. Everything in prison was reduced to a common denominator; no individualism, little communication, just a number. The plan was dehumanising, hoping supposedly to deter an inmate from re-offending but more often instilling a hatred for authority. The barber was an inmate called Lenny Lawson, the 'model man'. Lenny wasn't a model prisoner; he had earned the nickname for his crimes of murdering Sydney models. I got on well with Lenny because Lenny knew although I was young I wouldn't step down. I held my own against other inmates and helped other inmates debate issues with the Governor. Not so one prisoner, a middle-aged man, one ahead of me in the barber shop queue. He taunted Lenny, calling him names. When his turn came up for his haircut he had a go at Lenny again.

"Sit down," Lenny said and taking the scissors he stabbed him three times in the head, killing the man.

Lenny got another life sentence for that murder. He was already serving three life sentences anyway. Lenny was released in 1977 so he must have behaved himself after that.

I served one year of my one and a half year sentence being released six months early for good behaviour. I did come out with a determination not to return but I was not reformed. My prison experience had cemented in me a hatred for authority; so deep I even hated the colour blue.

8

GANGLAND DAYS

I was just short of twenty years old when I was released from Grafton Prison. Making my way to Sydney I found a job at a Masterfoods factory, loading cans of food into the big steamer. After hours I would go to the pubs looking for extra work. One night I was in the Balaclava Hotel at Redfern when a tough looking fellow strode into the pub and shot a man at point blank range while he was sitting in a chair. Picking up the dead man he carried him out of building and put him in the boot of a car.

"What about that black fella; he saw what happened," he hissed to his companion, Neddy Smith.

"Let him be, he's O.K."

The hit man approached me, "You never saw nothing that happened, right."

"I'm no dog," I responded.

To make his point the gunman grabbed me by the neck. That was the wrong move. Never a man to back down, I decked him. Neddy Smith recognised me as the young man who had been jailed for bashing coppers.

The big white man walked up to me, "You didn't see a thing," he said, handing me a wad of cash.

I knew Neddy Smith too, not personally, just by reputation, just as I knew a lot of gang members who operated the Redfern area, Waterloo and the Eastern Suburbs.

I saw an opportunity to make an easy dollar so I spoke up, "Mate, I need money and I'm willing to work."

"Be at the Bat and Ball tomorrow night, eight o'clock."

Arthur Stanley "Neddy" Smith was a stand over man. He was into everything; drugs, prostitution, armed robbery and murder. He also worked for the police, though I was unaware of that at first. Police were paid-off to overlook Neddy's illegal activities. At the Bat and Ball I found Neddy drunk, talking gibberish.

"Have a drink, mate," he offered.

"No thanks," I never had a drink in my life.

"Well, you can work for me."

So began an uneasy partnership. When the amber fluid loosed his tongue, which was often, Neddy would brag about his relationship with the police.

"I've got the green light," he would boast, "I can do whatever I want." And so it seemed.

My job was to drive Neddy's ute. Neddy and two other blokes were hiding in the tray until they were near the job. The men would draw guns on the guards of an armoured car, make the men lie on the ground and steal the cash. This happened many times in different locations; the Eastern Suburbs, Balmain and Chatswood. Later Neddy would meet up with a copper and pay him out. As the money rolled in I left my day-time job. I justified my new employment. I didn't deal in drugs or use them myself but I protected people who did. My good upbringing and religious principles were over-ridden by hatred for authority along with my love of fighting and the easy money.

Fights with other gangs were common. Neddy would take me along to fight anyone who was edging in on his turf. But even among thieves there was a code of honour; you could be an armed robber but still a good bloke. I was worried for a friend. The man had been involved in robberies and drug deals. He had upset Neddy by getting involved with a prostitute, Sally Anne.

I reasoned with my friend, "I wouldn't get in the car if I were you, walk away!"

Unfortunately my friend didn't listen.

Neddy came over.

"These are for you," he said, throwing a bank bag, balaclava and a shorn-off shot gun in the car. "Get lost you lousy......!"

My friend only got as far the next intersection where three waiting police cars, a squad led by Detective Rogerson, rammed his car. As my friend jumped out Roger Rogerson shot him with a blast from his shotgun. I realised that people were going missing, criminals yes, but good people and I was wondering if I might be next.

Today Neddy Smith is serving two life sentences in Long Bay Goal. On Thursday 11th December 2008 a report was broadcast by the ABC concerning Smith's request for early release.[1] Smith was described as a major drug dealer who also raised cash through armed hold-ups. On his criminal CV was drug-dealing, prostitute-running, rape, armed robbery and murder. He became a national figure when he later 'rolled over' and gave evidence against the police, whom he said gave him a green light to commit crime as long as they were not harmed. Neddy Smith named corrupt detectives, including Roger Rogerson. Rogerson was kicked out of the police force in 1986. He was reported as telling Radio 2GB's Alan Jones that politicians would be too scared to release such a high profile criminal.[2]

In the same ABC transcript, John Laylock, the now retired assistant police commissioner described Smith as a very ruthless person and heavily involved in the drug trade. Laylock said that there was a fair bit of competition in the drug trade and Smith decided the best way to get rid of competition was to take them out; which he did quite successfully. When asked how many people he thought Smith had killed Laylock replied that the force had looked at a total of fourteen cases of murder that Smith may have been involved in but at the end of the day he was only convicted on two counts. As well as the 1987 murder of tow-truck driver, Ronnie Flavell, Smith copped a second life sentence for the 1983 murder of brothel-keeper, Harvey Jones.

An article from in the Daily Telegraph December 11th 2008 described Smith in his heyday as 'almost 2m tall and built like the proverbial brick outhouse - could throw punches like an unstoppable "threshing machine"'.[3] Now Parkinson's disease has reduced Smith to a shaking wreck of a man but the authorities are still reluctant to release a man who was once one of the best known figures from Sydney's 1980's drug wars.

While working for Neddy, one incident stood out in my mind. Gang-land shootings were common-place. I was involved in a shoot-out involving a gang of bikies who were edging in on Neddy's turf. Neddy, myself and four of Neddy's men confronted four men from the bikie gang.

I warned the sergeant-in-arms, "Don't pass over the boundary, keep clear, or else."

Suddenly Neddy pulled out a piece and shot one of the bikies in the leg. A bikie responded by firing his shotgun into the air. As I was unarmed I ran to the car and grabbed a 410, a small shotgun. Shots were exchanged on both sides. As the bikies rode off I aimed at one of the motorbike wheels and its rider crashed to the ground. The others speed off. The man on the ground was bloodied from the fall and not moving.

Neddy handed me a pistol, "Finish him off."

As Neddy walked away I was thinking fast.

The fallen man begged, "Please mate, please I've got a family, please, I'm just like you."

"Don't move," I whispered, "do not move as I walk away."

I fired off four shots right next to the man's head then walked away.

I'm not a murderer. In my mind a murderer kills for the thrill of it. A soldier who kills a man is not thought of as a murderer is he? I've been found guilty of aggravated assault, possessing firearms, stealing and breaking and entering but I've never been convicted of murder and there will be no confession to any crime in these pages while I could still be indicted. While working for Neddy 'accidents' sometimes happened and to protect ourselves and our turf it was necessary to put some people 'to sleep' as we termed it. It was just part of the job. The 'victims' were policemen on the take or criminals like ourselves. At the time I felt no remorse, I'd put the killings in some deep dark recess of my mind but in later days they came to haunt me.

The last mass defection from the powerful motorcycle gangs led to the notorious Milperra massacre in 1984 when a breakaway group of Comancheros formed the first Bandidos chapter in Australia. The two outlaw biker clubs, the Comancheros and the Bandidos, engaged in a bitter feud intense for control of the cocaine trade and the manufacture and supply of amphetamines. On September 2, 1984 at the Viking Tavern in the Sydney suburb of Milperra, a violent shoot-out erupted in the hotel car park in full view of terrified members of the public resulting in the deaths of six bikies and a fifteen year-old girl. Leanne Waters had been selling raffle tickets at the front of the tavern where the fight broke out. Twenty more were wounded. William 'Jock' Ross, 'supreme commander' of the Comancheros and primarily responsible for the decision that members of his club go to Milperra in force and armed, received a life sentence. Several other members of the Comancheros received life sentences and sixteen Bandidos received sentences of fourteen years for manslaughter.[4]

Several of the gang members served their sentences in Long Bay Correctional Centre. These men were so scared of the other inmates that they would lock themselves in their cells. Later when I was serving time in the same jail I spoke to one of the men, the one they called Sunshine.

"Listen Bud, " I said, "it might be tough but there were innocent kids out there."

Sunshine replied, "We didn't want any trouble. It was an accident, but your face is familiar to me."

"We see each other most days here," I replied.

"No, that's not it, I know you."

Although the man's face was not familiar to me the incident bothered me; perhaps the man had something on me. I could not sleep at night for worrying about it. I persuaded the prison warden on his wing to take me to the bikie's cell.

"You seem a nice bloke, where do you know me from?" I asked.

"All I can say is when you're facing death and someone gives you a second chance, you never forget it".

I was dumbfounded. Weeks passed before we had opportunity for another chat.

"Explain to me what you were talking about, the other day," I demanded.

"You're a good man Charlie."

"If I was a good man I wouldn't be locked up," I retorted.

"There are good men in jail," Sunshine replied handing me a Bible.

"What's that for?" I asked backing away.

It always softened me when God was mentioned.

"Charlie I didn't kill any kids, I've got kids of my own. Sure, I'm in a bikie gang, but the gang went off the track, got into drugs. Really we all just wanted to ride to get away and feel the breeze. Anyway I just want to thank you; I'll never forget you saved my life."

At last I remembered the incident and Sunshine and I became good friends. Perhaps there are some good men in jail after all.

I was involved with Neddy Smith and Sydney gangland in the 1980's but I was still my own master. My life was saved by constantly moving back and forward from the bush. Much of the time no-one knew where I was. Also I could act the 'dumb nigger' from the sticks when I wanted to but in reality I was always thinking ahead and planning my movements.

......

1. *Early release ruled out for notorious 'Neddy' Smith*, Transcript from the World Today Program, ABC, 11.12.2008

2. *Early release ruled out for notorious 'Neddy' Smith*, Transcript from the World Today Program, ABC, 11.12.2008

3. *Killer Arthur 'Neddy' Smith pleads for mercy release*, The Daily Telegraph, 11.12.2008

4. www.bookrags.com/wiki/Milperra_massacre sighted 18.05.2009

9

CHARLIE'S WOMEN

"Hi," the pretty young woman greeted the man at the turnstile. "Do you know if Charlie Quinlan is here?"

The tall, slender girl had long black hair and strikingly green eyes.

The gate-keeper knew I was at the football match, but kept his face was impassive, "Dunno, whatcha want Charlie for?

"Well, I trying to find him, he's my Dad," she replied.

Theo laughed, "Sure, they all say that!"

"No, really Charles Quinlan is my father. Look, if you see him, give him my number, okay."

Theo took the proffered piece of paper and went in search of me.

"I just met a lady who reckons she's yer daughter, mate!"

Theo thought it was a great joke.

"Here," he said, handling me the paper, "here's 'er number; better give 'er a ring, eh."

Theo broke into another fit of laughter.

I didn't know what to do. I said nothing to my wife, Luana, but mulled over it for a couple of days before dialling the number. Bianca was a stewardess for Ansett Airlines. The next time her route took her to Sydney I met her at the airport. I scanned the faces, not recognising any one but one young lady immediately recognised me. I didn't know what to say.

I didn't even know who this woman's mother was, so I asked lamely, "How's your mum?"

"Oh, my mum Maria, she passed away a couple of years back."

Maria! Memories flooded back; Maria. After I'd saved a few hundred dollars, I had left the MacKay's. I had hitchhiked to Sydney. I hadn't said anything to Elva but rang when I got to Redfern, just to let her know I was fine. I was fifteen years old. I had no trouble finding a bed at Redfern as I had relatives living there and most folk would give a young boy a place to doss down, relative or not.

Maria was one of the prettiest girls around. I had met her hanging around the streets just like I was. She was from Melbourne, about my own age, just visiting like me. We'd chatted and exchanged names. Some weeks later she invited me to stay at her friend's house. It came as a huge shock to me when Maria told me she was pregnant. We argued.

"I'm too young and I haven't a job so how can I look after a kid?" I said, "You'll have to get rid of it."

Maria went back to Melbourne and we lost touch after that.

Looking at the young woman before me I remembered Maria's beautiful green eyes and I could see my own features in her too. I wondered, after all this time, how did she know who her father was. Bianca showed me her birth certificate, in bold print the name, **BIANCA QUINLAN**. Maria had given birth in Melbourne. Harbouring no ill feelings she had named her daughter using my surname. Bianca showed me a photograph of me and Maria, somewhat faded and marked by much handling, but still recognisable.

"That's how I recognised you at the terminal. Mum said you were the best looking guy in Sydney. I'm a Quinlan just like you; Mum wanted me to have your name. She always said you and her couldn't be together because you were too young and lived too far away."

I went cold all over. Bianca started to cry and we just hugged each other.

Bianca lives with her grandmother in Melbourne now but we have kept in touch. Maybe one day she'll meet my wife, Luana, and my other children. I had to tell Luana about Maria and Bianca but she took the news calmly. She's the one who wears my ring and it's all in the past.

After Maria left, I lived the life of a wanderer. Always a loner, I would hitch-hike back and forth from Sydney to Bellbrook, picking up work here and there. In those days a fit young man could walk onto a building site and ask for a job. Usually he would be taken on, to load bricks or clean up a site. In a few days I would move on. I learnt a lot of skills this way and I liked working with older men. Without my realising it the workmen took the place to some extent of the father and grandfather I had lost.

After I served my first jail sentence at the infamous Grafton Jail I stayed on at Grafton with my Uncle Raymond, working at Koppers Sawmill. Raymond was a Bellbrook boy and like my deceased father he also worked for the railways. June, Ray's blonde, blue-eyed sister-in-law was visiting and I fell in love. June also became pregnant, but this time, unknown to me, her sister fetched her and took her to Grafton hospital for an abortion. Even now June cries when she thinks about the loss of that baby. June's parents did not approve of me and the relationship suffered from their interference and my absences. June fell pregnant again, but I wasn't around and I was not informed. Later June told me that Bradley was our son and although I wasn't absolutely convinced a close relationship formed between me and Bradley.

During my fractured relationship with June, I met up with another blonde, a German girl named Cindy from Seven Hills. Of all my mother-in-laws I got on with Cindy's mother the best. She took the time to sit and talk with me. But I was set in a pattern in my relationships; as soon as a problem arose I would move on, returning to a previous woman when the new alliance hit a rocky patch.

Opportunity presented itself again at a job making bricks at Mirriwinni Gardens Aboriginal Academy near Bellbrook. A fourteen year old student at the school, Robyn Skinner liked the look of me. She was also attracted to my cousin Joe Quinlan. An uneasy threesome developed. I followed Robyn to Grafton, but after a row she would take off to Joe's place. As in my previous relationships when Robyn became pregnant I took off, frightened again as I always was when facing the responsibility of fatherhood and disappeared back to Cindy in Sydney.

As Cindy neared full term she became more and more demanding. I was working at a metal works and would come home dirty and greasy. Cindy insisted I wash before I lay down to rest.

One particularly demanding day, I told her, "I'm going to the shops for milk and bread," and was soon on the highway hitching my way north.

Arriving at Bellbrook my mother told me, "Son, you've got to get to Kempsey hospital, Robyn's baby's due."

Robyn had been staying with my mum in Bellbrook. I was pacing the waiting room when Amanda was born.

A few days later I was nursing 'Manda' in the maternity ward when the matron came in, "Where's Charlie Quinlan?"

"I'm Charlie," I admitted.

"Oh, I know you," the matron grinned, "I was present at your birth....," she paused, seemingly not sure how to deliver her message.

Taking the plunge she continued, "I've just had a call for you, you're to go back to Sydney. Your wife's just had a baby."

My long suffering mother looked at me aghast and Robyn grabbed Amanda.

"You've had a baby girl," the matron went on.

I turned all sorts of colours and left. The whole thing was a nightmare.

Back in Sydney I tried to be a father to all my children, visiting them, and continuing my relationships with the mothers. So began years of trouble. As the women quarrelled with me I would move around, trying to placate the 'wives' and children with gifts. Unable to resolve my feelings and having no-one to talk to I became argumentative and aggressive. My mother was busy raising her own large family and had problems of her own so I was determined not to burden her with my own woes. I felt I had no-one to turn to.

I knew I was responsible for the children and although I desperately wanted a family the women were unhappy with the situation so I never stayed with any one woman for long. To make matters worse I began an affair with another Aboriginal girl, Judy Craig from Coffs Harbour. When she too became pregnant I took her to her mother's house where Virginia was born. Later another daughter, Emily, was born.

My behaviour now followed a familiar pattern. I began spending time with another Coffs Harbour girl, Eileen Reilly. It wasn't a normal relationship because by this time I was on the run. Eileen followed me to Sydney where we would mostly meet on the street or in a café. Eileen was staying at Kerry Philip's home at Glebe. Another Eileen, Eileen Murray was dating Kerry's son, Greg. She accused Eileen Reilly of cheating on me with her boyfriend, so the pair swapped. Eileen Murray became the next in my long line of partners. She was still with me when I was interred in Long Bay Jail. My son and namesake, Charles Quinlan was conceived why I was in jail. Sadly, little Charlie died of cot death.

I was the acknowledged 'Aboriginal governor' of the remand centre. Although conjugal visits were forbidden, there was an underground section where more intimate visits could be bought at a price.

In late 1991 I started living with Luana. She was nineteen years old and although she had known me as a family friend for many years and knew I had been in jail, she did not really know the true extent of my crimes. I could not understand why she was attracted to me. Certainly her parents couldn't understand and were openly hostile. Luana's father was a pastor in a Pentecostal denomination. One difference between this relationship and the previous ones was this time I agreed to a legal marriage before any children were born.

Luana and Eileen, my previous partner, had a fragile relationship. While Luana was in hospital giving birth to Charlie Junior, her first child with me, Eileen was also admitted to the same hospital. Luana felt uneasy, even fearful for her first child, and discharged herself from hospital as soon as possible. Edward, Eileen's son was born three weeks later. When Luana discovered I had continued an affair with Eileen during our marriage she was distraught. Together the women concocted a plan to make me suffer.

There were two crimes that I would never tolerate; rape and crimes against children. Both women accused me of raping them. They expected me to get so angry I would become violent and end up in jail again. The case went to court. Eileen held to the lie but Luana, the pastor's daughter, could not bring herself to lie in court. In the end she refused to give evidence and I was worried she could be charged with false accusation. As neither women had been examined by a doctor and no evidence was proffered, the case was dismissed.

Eileen and I went to court to determine custody of our children, a daughter Tulla and younger child, Edward. Eileen was given custody of Tulla and I was given custody of Edward. Eileen and Luana have remained friends for the sake of the children. Although I was accused by some of my partners of domestic violence, Eileen testifies that I never hit her.

"He's a good man," she says, "and I still love him."

Today Luana and I have a strong marriage. We have ten children of our own. Some of my other children have been part of the family at different times. Of all the women I knew I definitely married the right one. Luana is patient, kind and forgiving. We love each other and she's the prettiest of them all.

10

DOUBLE TROUBLE

One incident involved my partner Robyn. Even though there were arguments with the women in my life I did not believe in hurting women. Some of the ladies would accuse me of domestic violence but it was just to hurt me by stopping me from seeing my children. Robyn had done just that. Consequently she was staying with my daughter Amanda at Robin's House, the women's refuge centre at Grafton. At Christmas, she contacted me and agreed for me to spend some time with Amanda. She instructed me to collect Amanda from the refuge.

My mum, Judith, advised me not to go.

"Don't try to force yourself on your children," she would say. "You'll get them in the end."

Judith was eventually proved right and I could have made things a lot easier for myself. Unfortunately, I ignored the advice.

I knocked on the door of the refuge centre.

When no-one opened the door I called out in a loud voice, "I'm here to pick up my daughter, Mandy. My wife's name's Robyn".

The door opened and a lady answered, "There's no-one here called Mandy or Robyn, you'd better be off," and slammed the door in my face.

I turned away angrily, thinking Robyn had set me up.

As I walked along the verandah I heard a small voice calling, "Daddy, Daddy."

Through the mesh I could see Amanda, who was about two years old. I knelt down, making baby noises to her. The woman who had answered the door grabbed Amanda by her dress, pulling her away before closing the screen.

As in the past, I lost all self-control. Regardless of the consequences, I ran back to my car, grabbed my shorn-off shot-gun, loaded 8 cartridges and blew the hinges off the front door. I ran inside, tucked Mandy under one arm and with murder on my mind went looking for the woman who had refused me. She had run out the back door and as she was jumping the fence I fired, blowing holes through the fence, twice just missing the woman. Amanda was screaming and within minutes sirens were blaring and the refuge was surrounded by policemen.

A voice over the loud speaker demanded, "Put the gun down; don't harm the girl."

I would not listen. All he could think of was iron bars and cement.

"She's my daughter, she's MY daughter," I sung out.

After about twelve attempts to persuade me to drop the weapon, I calmed down enough to throw the gun down. Immediately I was wrestled to the ground, kicked repeatedly in the face, handcuffed and taken to the 'local police station. There I was bashed with batons until the blood flowed. Blood was all over the place, even on the cell wall.

By this time the Aboriginal Legal Service had contacted the station to find out where I was but they were told I was not in custody. My mother contacted other lawyers who were able to obtain a court order to check the cells. Before the lawyers arrived the police tried to persuade me to clean myelf up but I refused. Due to the beating a deal was negotiated with the police. My sentence would be light if I didn't make a complaint against the police.

Oblivious to the drama that had taken place, Robyn had enjoyed a day at the beach. She had left a note on the notice board informing the refuge staff to release Amanda to my care that day but the notice board had not been checked.

A year later, on the 17th November 1985 I was committed for trial for abducting Judy Craig. Judy was the baby of her family; a fifteen year old Aboriginal girl, whose parents were not impressed with her infatuation with the twenty-three year old criminal, Charlie Quinlan. Against her parents wishes Judy phoned me and asked to come to her parent's home at Coffs Harbour. She wanted to run away with me.

I duly arrived in company with another man, Martin Wombat. Martin was driving his white Mazda RX4. He dropped me off around the corner from the house and parked in front of Judy's place. Seeing the car in front of her home, Judy came out.

"Where's Charlie?" she asked.

"He's just around the corner. He wants to see you." Martin replied.

So Judy jumped in the car, and Martin drove off, picking me up on the way.

Judy's parents rang the police, accusing me of dragging their daughter into a car. Later, their description of the our behaviour resulted in both Martin and I being charged with abduction and me with ill-treatment and common assault.

Near Bellingen the car battery went flat. We pushed the car into the bush and covered it with branches. Judy and I continued on foot in the bushland but Martin walked back to the road and was soon arrested. So began a massive manhunt.

Judy followed me walking through the bush towards Dorrigo. The weather was freezing, the creeks iced over and snow was falling intermittently. My mum was petrified we would die of exposure but we stayed alive cuddling up together at night for warmth.

After five days police spotted Judy on the top of a hill near a dirt track. I heard cars coming and ran off.

Judy chased after me singing out, "Wait for me, wait for me."

Our mad stampede ended at the edge of a gorge. With no other way of escape I began the perilous climb down the steep slope. Judy was determined to stay with me. She followed me down, slipped and fell on top of me. We both landed in a heap after a fall of about ten metres. Exhausted we lay there for a couple of hours. Judy couldn't keep up the pace so I carried her. Crossing an icy river she slipped again and the two of us were washed three hundred metres down the river before I could pull her out.

About ten o'clock at night we could see lights. I estimated we were about four kilometres from Dorrigo. All this time the radio was broadcasting about the 'abducted' girl never saying anything about her being my girlfriend.

At first light I started towards Dorrigo, carrying Judy on my back. On the outskirts of town I saw an old, white Holden HQ utility. Jiggling the lock I started the engine and drove to Kempsey. Just before North Street in West Kempsey was a road block. Seeing the Holden utility, the police drove their cars across the road. I slid the car into a bank and jumped out. It was dark so the police trained their headlights on me. I could hear the bullets whistling past me. I was also armed, carrying a pistol and a small sawn-off shotgun. Aiming at the headlights, the bullets found their mark and in the darkness I ran off.

Sergeant Smith was in command of the road block. As I was firing he was taking cover between two police vehicles. Years later, after I was finally released from Long Bay Jail I met him in the street.

"I wasn't trying to kill you Charlie, I was firing over your head," Smith told me.

"I'd 'ave shot you if I could've," I replied. "Thank God I missed."

Sometime later I was arrested and charged with abduction, assault and possession of a prohibited firearm. The following Coffs Harbour Advocate newspaper article is an indication of just how wrong the police could be. Firstly Judy had entered the car of her own free will and secondly my brother Ralph was not involved in the affair at all. Police often made the incorrect assumption that Ralph and I committed crimes together. In this case no crime was committed and the other man in the car was Martin Wombat.

Unfortunately for me, when I was eventually arrested I was found guilty of the lesser charge of possession of an illegal firearm. Judy testified that I was not in the Holden when she got into the car and I was not at any time trying the grab her screaming from her parent's house and every time I ran off she testified she was running after me which cleared me of the abduction charge.

A young and tough Charlie

The following article appeared in The Advocate 18th November 1985:

Abduction charge

A 23-year-old Port Macquarie man was refused bail by the magistrate, Mr Michael Doring, when he appeared in the Kempsey Local Court yesterday accused of the abduction of a 15-year-old Coffs Harbour girl on Sunday.

Charles Frederick Quinlan, of Douglas Street in Port Macquarie, was also charged with the possession of a prohibited weapon, an Armalite rifle, which the police allege he has had in his possession for several months.

The court was told that Quinlan went to the aid of his younger brother who was trying to remove the screaming girl from a house on the Wongala estate in Coffs Harbour. Quinlan was arrested in Bellbrook, near Kempsey, and the police are still looking for his brother.

The police prosecutor, Sergeant Frank Mahoney, opposed bail for Quinlan, who was represented by Mr Paul Stubbs, on the grounds that he would try to interfere with witnesses, that he was on remand for other offences and that he had previously failed to appear in court.

A detective with the Kempsey criminal investigation branch, Senior Constable Warwick Brown, told the court that Quinlan was a person with a complex about the television character, Mr T, and that he liked to dress in army style trousers, shirt, cap and boots.

Quinlan was remanded in custody and will appear again on December 9.

I wouldn't say I had a complex about Mr T. but there are some similarities between myself and Mr. T (Laurence Tureaud). He was a black man who came from a family of 12 children. He played football and worked as a bodyguard as I did. In the 1980's television series, 'A-team', Mr T played Sergeant Bosco 'B.A.' Baracus (B.A. is an abbreviation of 'Bad Attitude' as well as "Bosco Albert"), an ex-army commando on the run with three other members from the U.S. government 'for a crime they didn't commit.'

When asked at a press conference whether he was as stupid as B.A. Baracus, Mt. T observed quietly, "It takes a smart guy to play dumb."[1]

I was a black, powerful man and had a reputation for being tough and fearless. I always thought things through but could play the 'dumb nigger from the bush' when it suited me. However, I never took on Mr. T's mohawk hairstyle or penchant for wearing many gold neck chains and bracelets.

My frustration with Judy's parents resulted in a violent show-down. I hid in the garden of their Coffs Harbour home. When the parents came home I forced my way into the house. Judy's father fired at me with a 22 but the bullet missed and lodged in the wall. I disarmed him, hit him over the head with the gun and tied up the whole family except Judy.

When mother, father, sister and an auntie were restrained, Judy said to me, "Don't hurt them."

To her parents she pleaded, "Just leave us alone."

Her mother replied, "If you want to go with him, go, but don't ever come back here again."

Judy and I left together and set up house in Sydney.

We weren't to be left in peace. After returning from work I saw men in vests near our house. One of them knocked on the door.

When Judy opened the door a detective asked, "Is Mrs. Craig here?"

"Yes, I'm Judy Craig," Judy answered.

One of the detectives took Judy to their car. Pointing guns at me the policeman forced me to lie on the floor face down.

"What's going on?" I demanded.

"You know," was the reply accompanied by a hit on the head with the butt of a gun.

I had no idea why I was being arrested. I was handcuffed and escorted to a paddy wagon. At the station, I would not answer any questions or even admit who I was. I kept asking what I was arrested for and was getting very angry. A detective removed the handcuffs.

"You're being charged with kidnapping and murder."

"What!" I grabbed the police typewriter and threw it at the detective's head.

Police retaliated with batons. As on previous occasions, I went berserk, hardly feeling the policemen's blows. One policeman got a baton around my neck trying to drag me into a cell, but I kicked the man between his legs, jumped the counter and ran out of the station knocking the glass door right off its hinges.

At the first stoplight I pulled a man out of his car and drove into the bush at the back of Campbelltown. This incident earned me the nickname '*Rambo*' so called after the movie scene depicting a fight between policemen and a falsely arrested Vietnam veteran.

Judy's father died a year later. I had no idea what he died from but someone had decided I was to blame. Just as I was proven innocent of the abduction charge so I was proven innocent of the murder charge.

......

1. http://en.wikipedia.org/wiki/Mr._T sighted 01/06/2009.

11

ON THE RUN

I was now a wanted man. My altercations with police involved exchange of gunfire and the police were determined to track me down. When it became too hot for me on the coast I would head for Sydney where I had a lot of relatives who would give me a bed and ask no questions.

The police got cleverer closer to Sydney. South of Taree, a police car passed me on the Pacific Highway. The driver did not sound his siren this time but I knew he would be radioing ahead so I turned around following the police car from a distance. Before the police knew it, I was back at the Aboriginal community at Purfleet, Taree. Leaving the stolen Monaro in Purfleet I changed to a white Holden Commodore, hired by my friend Martin. The car was unusual; it had only one number plate. Was it a set-up?

Martin, myself and another friend Charlie Marr only got as far as Coolongolook before being spotted and chased by a police car, no subterfuge this time, sirens blaring. The Commodore was forced off the road near a Caltex service station. On this occasion the army had been called in and a scuffle ensued. One of the soldiers grabbed little Charlie Marr. Another soldier grabbed me by my shirt. I took off minus the shirt and raced into the thick scrub. However the place was a trap with the Manning River ahead and a creek between me and freedom. The army had over thirty men plus dogs.I ran to the creek and lay flat against its steep bank. From my hiding place I could hear every word of the men searching for me.

"He hasn't crossed the creek nor has he crossed the Manning River or we would have seen him," one said.

"We'll form a line men and scour the bush 'til we find him; shoot on sight," instructed their leader.

I waited quietly for about ten minutes. By this time I could hear the sounds of a helicopter and a plane making passes over the area. Ducking under the water in the creek, I removed all my clothes. Surfacing I came out of the water and ran through the bush to the Manning River. Hiding amongst shrubs I watched the helicopter make a pass over the river then a few minutes later the plane passed. Three times I attempted to cross the Manning but each time had to swim back when the plane appeared. The fourth time I made it across. Finding a hollow log I hid my head in the log with my body submerged in the water. The helicopter slowly hovered over the water, its pilot looking for bubbles, but seeing nothing, flew off.

By this time it was getting dark and the mozzies were savage so I plastered myself with clay before running back to Taree, all the while keeping to the mountains. The police were forced to try a new strategy. My uncle, Darryl Wright was an Aboriginal Liaison Officer. The police brought him to the area and gave him a horse in an attempt to track me down.

The following report appeared in the Macleay Argus:

Police Call in Tracker Dogs

Police are using tracker dogs in the search for a desperate fugitive who has fled to the bushland south of Taree.

The former Bellbrook man has led the police on a wild chase from Port Macquarie to Kempsey, Armidale and Macksville since Wednesday. He was armed and believed to be dangerous until narrowly escaping police without his weapons on Friday.

Police sighted the 26-year-old man and his two accomplices as they made their way south through Coolongolook late Friday afternoon and a desperate movie-style car chase began through the unsealed back roads of the forest.

The drama continued for some minutes before the men's borrowed white Commodore sedan was forced off the road and police swooped. They actually grabbed the solidly built Aboriginal man by the shirt but as he struggled it ripped from his body and he fled into the bush.

However his companions, two Kempsey men aged 23 and 17, were arrested and are charged with motor vehicle theft. Police tracker dogs and Pol-air helicopter were bought in from Sydney and by Saturday were sweeping the bushland of the Coolongoolook forests.

It is thought the man is now unarmed after leaving behind his rifle, stolen machetes, camouflage clothing and camping gear in the car.

His 20-year-old brother was not with fugitives, as first thought by police. He is also wanted in relation to dishonesty crimes.

Search commanding officer, Detective Sergeant Bob Williams said the man's luck has to run out soon.

Police thought the men would continue to Sydney after being sighted heading south in a stolen red Monaro early Friday. It is believed they sought refuge in Purfleet, on theoutskirts of Taree. It is also suspected they were given the white Commodore by a Purfleet woman to carry on their flight from police.

Police say the fugitive will be scared and searching for help. Det Williams is urging all people sighting or hearing of the man to contact police immediate-ly.[1]

About a kilometre out of Taree I came across a house. I had no clothes and was cold and hungry. I knocked on the door but no-one was home. Apparently the owner worked for Australia Post as the Australian Post uniform was hanging on the washing line. What a bit of luck! Quickly

I changed into the uniform and taking an Australia Post bag I hid near Taree railway station. Late at night a goods train came through. Running alongside, I jumped the train and got a lift right to Newcastle.

From there I boarded a passenger train. Exhausted I fell asleep, to be woken up by an old lady sitting next to me.

"Is this your stop Sonny?" she asked, "Don't forget to deliver my mail."

Another train took me to Redfern. As I walked down the main street of Redfern some children recognised me.

"Hey, do you know you're on TV?" they said, "you're Australia's most wanted man!"

I stayed with Theo and George Smith in Redfern. Both men worked for Railway Security. They were not really family but Theo later married one of my cousins. My name was splashed all over the television. I was really fidgety in Sydney; I only felt at ease in the bush. The slugs I'd been hit with, in my escape from police at Port Macquarie, were still causing me pain and the wounds bleeding.

I had opportunity to have those slugs removed at a later date in a prison hospital but a lawyer warned me that other things might happen to me while under anaesthetic; if a nerve was damaged I could come out a cripple. Due to my distrust of authority those seven pellets are still in my back today. After a few days at Redfern I moved to Kerry Phillips place at Glebe. While there something happened to make things really confusing for me.

An aboriginal man, from Queensland, his hair in dreadlocks, decided to do a job at Hyde Park in the city, an armed robbery. His name was John Porter. While he was stealing a car to do the job, he was spotted by two detectives who approached him to ask him what he was doing. When the police tried to search him John ran off because he had a gun on him. Even though Johnny was carrying a weapon for the robbery I'm sure he had no bullets for the gun or even a firing pin in the gun.

As John ran off the two detectives started firing. The younger policeman, Alan McQueen, ran faster than his partner. As John Porter jumped down a gutter, Alan fell and Johnny got away. McQueen had been shot and later died in hospital, the bullet apparently going through his back and out the front of his body. John Porter got life for killing the policeman. He's still serving his time at Lithgow Prison. He was a criminal, a petty thief, but Johnny says he never killed that policeman. Despite the lack of evidence the court case went against him. I reckoned the police had it all tied up; policemen are trained, it was claimed, so they couldn't accidentally shoot each other.

Police records tell a completely different story. On the morning of 24 April, 1989, Constable McQueen, Constable First Class Ross Judd and Probationary Constable Jason Donnelly were patrolling the Woloomooloo area. All were members of the District Anti-Theft Squad. Around 11:35 a.m. they saw the offender Porter, apparently attempting to break into a motor vehicle. While Constable Judd parked the Police vehicle, Constables McQueen and Donnelly went to speak to the offender. As he was being detained, the offender produced a concealed weapon and shot Constable McQueen twice in the chest and Constable Donnelly in the abdomen. Both Constables then chased the offender, who continued firing at them, until both collapsed from their wounds. Constable Ross Judd also pursued and fired at the offender before returning to assist his colleagues. He then carried both wounded Constables to the Police car and drove them to the Sydney Hospital. Constable Donnelly was to recover from his wounds, however Constable McQueen had sustained extensive internal injuries and died on 5 May, 1989. The offender was later arrested by Queensland Police.[2]

Sitting in the Glebe house I heard the thud, thud, thud of the helicopter blades overhead.

"They've traced me," I thought.

Glancing through the window I saw armed police coming up the road, searching house by house. At some houses they knocked on the door, at others they just smashed the door. I realised this was the Tactical Response Group (TRG). I grabbed my 2 pistols pushing one in the front and the other in the back of my trousers.

"Get Uncle George's security uniform," I ordered a young fella in the house.

George and I were about the same build. The TRG were only two doors away. Both myself and Theo dressed in railway security uniforms complete with batons.

"I'm going out with a big bang," I said, "I'm going to take these fellas on."

"No, no," Theo said. "Keep calm, get in the car and let me do the talking."

Straightaway the officers came over to the car.

"What's the problem officer?" Theo asked in a cool manner.

"Open up the boot," ordered one of officers.

Theo got out and opened the boot.

"Tip your hat."

Theo took off his hat. An officer tapped the side window where I sat.

"Tip your hat". I was shaking but I took my hat off.

"Okay, you're right to go."

On the very next corner they were stopped once again.

The same thing, "Open the boot, tip your hat."

I was getting a bit cocky now.

"We've just had the same thing down the road. You're holding us up; we're late for work."

Arriving at Marrickville we turned on the news to hear that the police were looking for an Aboriginal fellow with dreadlocks. Apparently he'd shot a policeman. The hunt went on; helicopters, house searches. I don't know if they ever found the man.

A sad event at this time was the death of David Gundy. 'In one of these raids, David Gundy was shot dead by the police Special Weapons and

Operations Squad (SWOS). SWOS claimed they had information that John Porter was at the house, but in fact he was not. David was asleep in bed at home when they kicked in the door and blasted him to death. SWOS officers were also to claim that David grabbed the shotgun carried by Constable Dawson as it pointed at him, and it went off inadvertently. Few people believed this ridiculous story. Public anger grew with the realisation that David had been killed in his own bedroom at night and the police would not even apologise or admit they'd done anything wrong. The killing of innocent David Gundy sparked a furore, especially as there was already an ongoing Royal Commission into more than a hundred Aboriginals deaths in custody, over the past decade. There were organised protests, before and after David Gundy's funeral....As Police Minister Ted Pickering had immediately sympathised with the police involved, saying they were understandably 'uptight' and 'edgy', he became the target of public criticism...State Coroner Kevin Waller said he would hear an inquest into the death, and called for an end to comments over the shooting. However Royal Commissioner Hal Wootten said the case would also come within the terms of the death in custody Royal Commission, and that he would look at it when Waller's inquest was finished. Waller went on to conclude that no police officer had done anything wrong, and recommended that police in future be given more powers to forcibly enter private premises. Wooten's inquiry was critical of the police raid, but did not suggest any criminal charges.' [3]

I thought, "I've got to get out of Sydney".

If I'd known Johnny Porter was heading for Queensland I would have gone the other way but I only had thoughts of my cave, the one place I felt safe.

Of all my sisters Lena was the gamest. She and her boyfriend drove me as far as Newcastle before being forced back by roadblocks. I was asleep in the back seat and Lena's boyfriend was driving when we came upon a roadblock near Gosford. Lena's boyfriend was not too smart; he was slowing down to stop.

"What are you doing, you stupid idiot, go, go, go!" I screamed.

The car crashed through the roadblock and as it skidded around a sharp corner I opened the door and dived out in a big briar bush which cut me up a bit. The police followed the car and took Lena and her boyfriend to the Police Station. Unfortunately, I had left my guns in the car.

"Whose guns are these?" the officer demanded. "What's your name?"

When Lena said she was Lena Quinlan they realised too late who had been in the car. A massive manhunt ensued. Two men were on the loose, one a cop killer and the other one who would kill a cop if he could.

Soon the highway was packed with police cars. I was hiding in the bush. A truckie stopped to check his tyres and I jumped on the back of the truck gripping onto some of the rope used to tie down the canvas top. I thought I would die on that trip. The canvas was flying up and down, tossing me back and forth like a rag doll as the truckie sped on at insane speeds of over one hundred and forty kilometres per hour. At a red light I thankfully jumped off and made my way back to Glebe. I definitely should have gone south.

......

1. Macleay Argus, *Police call in tracker dogs*, Tuesday November 22nd 1988, reporter Vanessa Kenney

2. www.policensw.com/info/policerem/text/index22.html sighted 10.03.09

3. *lorikeet.and.com.au/t2/B3-POLRC.htm* sighted 08.01.09

12

LENA

My sister Lena was born when the family lived at Kundabung. It was time of great stability in her life. Her father Ralph provided for the family's needs, not spending money on frivolous items but on things of value such as Christian books. She remembers the days beginning with her mother and the children sitting in the lounge sharing family time with God. The children had their favourite songs and stories from Uncle Arthur's Bedtime Stories. Dad had already gone to work.

After breakfast she would walk with her mother and the older siblings to the highway to meet the bus taking the children to the Adventist school at Port Macquarie. The rest of the day she had Mum to herself but the highlight was Dad's return home. Lena knew the sound of the big green truck he drove and everyday she would run outside to welcome her father home. Ralph would grab the youngest boy, hoisting him on his broad shoulders, then carry Lena in his arms to the house. After dinner the family gathered together for worship before bed. The days followed a set routine, comfortable and safe.

Although only young, Lena remembers the day Dad died of the heart attack even though she didn't really understand what was happening at the time. She remembers sister Michelle, playing with the next youngest, Jenny, on the lawn and Mum doing the washing. Dad had been lying down in the car while Lena was entertaining herself, running to him for moment, leaning on his stomach then dashing back up the stairs to Mum in the laundry. Back and forth she would go when suddenly she heard the sounds of sirens and people crying and yelling. She had thought Dad was asleep with the Bible on his chest. Her Mum went in the ambulance with Dad and she was in the car following. The cousin driving the car did not have a licence and was very small so they had to get a tyre out of the boot for her to sit on so she could see through the windscreen. After Dad died her happy, comfortable and orderly life changed.

Dad had purchased a house in Kundabung, far away from the Aboriginal Reserve. Perhaps that is the reason some things happened after he died. When the family returned home from the funeral relatives had taken some of their furniture and other belongings. Lena did not know if these things belonged to them or they were taken out of spite. Ralph's death certificate stated his father was unknown. These things bothered Lena.

When she was older and was living at Port Macquarie most Friday afternoons after school she would catch a bus to Kempsey to stay with relatives so she could worship at the Kempsey Aboriginal Seventh-day Adventist church. One Sabbath, while walking down Yarravel Street on the way to church, she passed some people yarning on the verandah of a house.

An elderly gentleman called her over in a firm but gentle voice, "S'cuse me, can you come 'ere a minute?"

Lena answered, "Are you speaking to me?"

"Yeah,'" he replied.

As Lena walked slowly through the gate she looked into his eyes, feeling an immediate connection as though she was looking at a familiar face.

"Are you Ralph and Judith's daughter?" the old man asked.

"Yes, I am," Lena proudly answered.

"Do you know who I am?" he asked.

Lena did not know.

Her older siblings knew more of their relatives than she did, being the youngest, but she had been brought to answer politely so she replied, "No, I'm really sorry. I don't know who you are."

He began to answer, "I'm your....," then hesitated as if unsure how to proceed, but he finished his sentence, "....your grandfather."

Perhaps that is why some relatives took things; there must have been bad feelings, but in Lena's eyes there was not better man born than her father. Even now, with children of her own, she really misses him. Lena's life may have been very different if her father had not died.

Our mother sold the house at Kundabung and moved back to Bellbrook Reserve. Lena was upset; that house was her Dad's blood, sweat and tears, their little haven of security and protection from the problems at the Bellbrook Reserve and with relatives. However there was nothing she could do about it; she was too young. While living on the Reserve Lena attended the public school in the little township of Bellbrook.

The reserves were an Australian government idea about which the native people had no say. My people were a nomadic people, busy, living off the land. Now we were confined to a small area of ground with rules and regulations and no meaningful employment especially for the young people. We were losing our ancestral roots nor did we fit into white society.

This in her own words is Lena's story.

I remember having a good day at school, feeling happy until the time came to board the bus for the Reserve. As soon as the bus bumped over the grid before entering Bellbrook Reserve I would start praying. Next, I would beg my cousins to come home with me to play dress-ups or bake a cake; anything to have some company especially if I knew my Mum had gone to Kempsey for the day.

Mostly my cousins would say, "Nah, we've gotta go home."

The first stop was the Toby's, the second stop mine, the house with the big jacaranda tree at the front.

My eyes would be closed tight, then as the children sang out, "Come on Lena, it's your stop," I would open my eyes hoping, wishing to see my mother's car.

If the car wasn't there my stomach would feel like a stone weight, my heart pumping and a huge fear would descend upon me.

My feelings on those days were such as no child should have to deal with. I would quickly enter through the back door of our house, nervous as cornered deer. I'd take out five knives from the kitchen drawer and push them at the edges of the door to force it closed. After changing out of my school uniform, I'd get something to eat and sit close in front of the television, the volume turned down low, hoping no-one would think anyone was in the house.

Perhaps an hour or so later, I would hear footsteps coming up the path. Immediately I would turn off the television and hide under my bed. There would be a knock on the front door. He was clever, checking first to see if anyone was there. If there was no answer the footsteps would go to the back door; bang, bang, bang. I would be counting the knives as they fell, one.. two.. three..... Too often they all fell and I knew it was not someone coming on a friendly visit. A boy would find me and rape me. I was about ten at the time. The perpetrators were men and boys on the Reserve; teenagers or men in their early twenties.

I was not the only one. When one of my cousins died I cried bitterly for her as I knew she too had been raped as a child and had two children to her abuser. I never said anything. I was too disgusted, ashamed and scared. My abusers threatened me if I ever said anything so I kept quiet as did the other girls. Some of these boys used to come over to visit my brothers. It made me feel sick to see them with my brothers. The secret was held tightly to my heart all throughout my childhood, teens, high school and into adulthood. It affected my own relationships; I would not consider a man of my own kind. Now I have told my mother and siblings, as well the author of this book, because people should know and telling is healing.

I was disgusted when Lena told me of her abuse. Too long ago. And who knows, if I hadn't been the big bloke that girls both black and white fancied I could have been guilty of the same thing. The truth is one time I saw a white girl behind Woolworths at Kempsey. No-one was around and I raped her because she was white and I was angry. That was the only time. I was never called to account for that crime. I suppose she was too scared or ashamed and never contacted the police. I've had so many women and fathered 19 children, 9 out of wedlock so I'm just as bad.

It was difficult for me to express myself over the death of my father but as Lena's life went to pieces, so too did mine. All the siblings coped in different ways. For a while, the older children were sent to Mirriwinni Gardens Aboriginal Academy, an Aboriginal boarding school about an half hour's drive from the Reserve. I spent a couple of years with the MacKay family while my older sister Sharon stayed with relatives at Armidale.

When Sharon moved to Port Macquarie with her partner Peter, a white man, Lena saw her opportunity to escape.

Sharon asked Lena, "We're moving to Port, would you like……..".

Lena finished the sentence for her, "I knew you were going to ask me. Yes, yes, yes!"

"You'll have to ask Mum first," said Sharon.

That would be easy Lena, thought. She would beg her if necessary. When Lena was given her ticket to freedom, she knew she was going to be a different person, not bound to those boys' pleasures. She would be able to come and go as she pleased. Lena thought she was ready to face anything and she had a lot to face. She was a little black girl from a country reserve going to a big town and surrounded by white people.

Lena was enrolled in Port Macquarie Public School, determined to be on her best behaviour and never miss a day. As the only black girl in the school, for the first time she had to deal with the ugly face of racism but it was nothing compared to what she endured on the Reserve and she was determined. Lena was mocked for her poor English, she was called, 'boong', 'coon' and 'abo'. The racism was never ending. Lena was there to get an education and she objected to being constantly reminded where she came from.

When students hit her Lena would chase them and fight back and her tormentors would run to the teachers for protection. The teacher would always ask the white students what had happened first but Lena would reply first, telling the truth. She got by in primary school by being good at sports and fighting those who fought her.

By high school she had become more confident. After one fight the principal and teachers asked her how they could help her. Lena replied she would like to educate them about her people so her teachers allowed her to do her work with an Aboriginal emphasis. She wrote Aboriginal poems and stories, drew Aboriginal art and wrote about Aboriginal history and geography. During class she would read her work to the other students.

Lena was known as the youngest daughter but there was another girl born two years after her, Berryl Grace Quinlan, named after her father's sister, Aunty Berryl. When Judith gave birth to Berryl at Port Macquarie hospital, she was in hospital for a few days longer than normal as she was unwell.

During this time she met two white women who lived near the hospital and used to visit the nursery. Her husband Ralph was still alive at this time. The day the nurses said the baby should go home no-one had bought any clothes for the baby. It was not that they didn't have any clothes at home but welfare was very strict and perhaps they thought the family could not afford any baby clothes. One of the white women, Lola Hayes, overhead the conversation and offered to look after baby Berryl for a few days. Ralph and Judith thanked her for her kindness and Judith returned home without Berryl.

When the family went to collect Berryl, Lola pleaded to keep the baby a bit longer as she and her daughter had fallen in love with her. So Berryl stayed with Lola a little longer. Soon after Ralph died and Lola suggested Berryl stay with her until Judith had finished grieving and got on her feet.

This stretched on for months until Lola did not want to give the baby back at all. Judith was struggling with the seven children and had no idea how to get her baby back; certainly she was ignorant of the court system so Berryl remained with Lola and was renamed Chantelle Jade Hayes. As Lena grew up she would beg to see her little sister, buy her a birthday present or talk to her on the phone. She could not understand why her little sister was somewhere else. Judith would shop for a present and take Lena to visit Chantelle. Later when Lena had her own children Chantelle stayed with Lena in her Campbelltown home. Lena always wanted to show Chantelle love as the older sister, to show her that she was part of the family, from the same womb whether Chantelle liked it or not.

During the time Lena lived with Sharon, I was a young man doing my own thing. I had a nice set of wheels and had avoided serious trouble with the police. I used to visit my sisters and ended up renting the unit next to them on the first floor. It was at this time I had the relationship with Robyn Skinner, a young girl I met at Mirriwinni Gardens Aboriginal Academy. Trouble began after a daughter was born, Amanda Gay Quinlan. Robyn was also seeing another boy, Joe, and there was lot of talk going on. From Lena's perspective Robyn would take off with Amanda and used the baby girl as a wedge against me. Robyn accused me of domestic violence and would seek refuge in a women's shelter. From her own experience Lena knew that I suffered from the loss of his grandfather and father. It was no excuse but the losses played a big part in my problems.

As I got into trouble, Lena always felt that the police had it in for me; tracking me down like a dog over petty things. Consequently she was the one whom I called on when I needed help. She would shop for me and bring me food. First she had to drive around making sure she was not being followed then meet me at a pre-determined location in the bush, such as Georges Creek on the back road to Armidale, or pick me up to take me to a safe house. Sometimes I would ring my mother but Lena was the one who would go.

One occasion when I was on the run I called Lena for a lift to Sydney. Lena responded as usual. She and her first partner, a Fijian boy named Kalaveti, picked me up and headed south. Lena was eighteen years old and Kalaveti seventeen. I was asleep in the back of the car, Lena resting in the passenger seat with Kalaveti driving.

Before dozing off Lena warned Kalaveti, "Take it easy, we don't want to alert the police. Wake me up if you get tired."

As we approached Gosford, just before the Merimba turnoff on the old Pacific Highway, there was a roadblock where police were conducting random breath tests. I woke up and growled at Kalaveti to drive through the roadblock, which he did, then I hissed at him to slow down. As the car slowed I jumped out, leapt over a fence and took off.

Once I was in the bush I was invisible. I had bought a bag with me but in my haste I had left it in the car.

As the police cars chased them, Lena said to Kalaveti, "Don't say that was my brother, say he was a hitchhiker we picked up."

When Kalaveti stopped the car, they were surrounded by police cars. The police picked up the bag and saw it contained a gun and a machete.

"Are these yours?" they asked.

"No," Lena replied truthfully. "It belongs to the man who leapt over the fence."

"Who is he?" they demanded.

"Some joker we picked up. He jumped out before we stopped," Lena lied.

In the beginning the police believed their story but still took them to Gosford for questioning. Lean and Kalaveti both stuck to the same story so the police took them to different rooms for questioning.

Kalaveti smiled and waved as he went to his room but later when the door opened he was slouched over, moaning. His head was down and he would not look at Lena so she knew he had been beaten up and told the real story. Lena did not blame him; it was the first time he had been exposed to anything like this. Lena gave them her real name but at first the police, being Gosford men, did not make the connection with Charlie Quinlan. Once they made the link questioning began in earnest.

Lena and Kalaveti were arrested at 3:00 a.m. and were eventually released in the afternoon without their car. They walked to Gosford Railway Station only to be re-arrested before the train came.

"If only we had caught a train," Lena thought.

Back at the police station Kalaveti was being given food but not Lena so she realised they had him talking well. Both were charged with possession of prohibited firearms and weapons.

Eventually Len's mother became aware of their predicament and contacted some friends who got them out of the police station. The whole affair was embarrassing and humiliating for Lena. She had to report to the police three days a week for months. This really upset her but she accepted that what I was going through was a lot worse. I was still her big brother whom she loved and respected.

13

INVASION DAY

I was still on the run, hiding out with friends in Sydney. The following day, a Friday, was a big day at Alexandria Park. While white Australians celebrated Captain Cook's landing at Botany Bay, we, Aboriginals, got together at Alexandra Park protesting the 'invasion'.

"There'll be thousands of black fellas down there, no-one will know you; great feed," my friends said.

It was true, the park would be packed with Aboriginals coming from all over the state not just Redfern. Against my better judgment I was talked into accompanying my friends. At the park I was enjoying himself, spending time with my daughter Mandy and my brother Ralph but there was something that made me feel uneasy about the place. I claimed I could sense the presence of policemen whether they were in uniform or not.

Suddenly I spotted Darryl Wright. Darryl was my uncle but he also worked for the police. He was looking straight at me so I lifted my shirt slightly to show I was carrying a 'piece'.

I've got to get out of here, I thought, " I don't trust that fella. I shouldn't have come. Australia's most wanted man showing his face in public, I must have been mad."

It was a set-up. The police had positioned men with scopes in houses around the park. As I jumped into a car with my daughter Mandy, police cars roared into the park; Tactical Response Group again.

One man jumped out of his car with a semi-automatic and took aim. I pushed Mandy to the floor of the car. When I looked up I could not see any police. Perhaps they had run for cover thinking I was going to shoot. One young chap ran toward the car shouting and waving his gun. I opened the door, hitting him with it.

I picked up the officer's gun but Mandy was screaming, "No Dad! No Dad!"

So I threw the gun under the car and ran into the crowd. The same young man I'd hit with the car door pulled a pistol out of his leg pocket, jumped up and chased me into the crowd. He was out of his mind, shooting wildly into the crowd.

I saw kids dropping to the ground and I turned round to face the madman. At that point he shot me. The bullet hit my index finger and deflected into my upper thigh. As he was trying to reload, my brother Ralph hit him on the jaw. As soon as the young man dropped to the ground the crowd went berserk, kicking him in the head until he was unconscious.

That policeman was lucky to survive. At the court hearing he claimed he had never fired his gun but slugs from his gun were found on the ground with a metal detector. No-one was charged over the incident. After the hearing he retired. The young man had not been in his right mind, perhaps hyped up with drugs before the operation.

In the confusion at the park I crawled on the ground to a nearby tip truck, owned by the Aboriginal community at Redfern. Children who knew me thought it was a lark and jumped on the back of the truck. They began to panic when I drove away from the park so I stopped at a corner store to buy icy poles to calm them down. Police driving past were unaware who it was who was driving the tip truck.

I drove to Uncle Victor's place in Petersham where my brother Ralph caught up with me. Ralph arranged for me to go to a Chinese doctor in Canterbury Road, Dulwich Hill.

"We need a favour", my cousin said to the doctor as he handed over a couple of hundred dollars.

"What do you want?" the doctor asked.

"This man's been shot," was the answer.

At that the doctor panicked.

"This has to be reported." he whimpered.

"Get the bullet out or get a bullet yourself!"

With shaking hands the doctor removed the bullet and dressed my finger.

I was angry with Darryl Wright. I reasoned he should not have alerted the police or he should have at least come over to talk to me; after all he was family. I was determined to kill him.

My cousin Paul was staying at Darryl's home when Ralph and I came to pay Darryl an unexpected visit. Paul called me his uncle out of respect. As a youngster he had been warned about getting involved with me but Paul's passion was football so he never got into trouble with the us. Nevertheless, he admired me because I was a strong, tough man who never drank or smoked. I could be depended on to get a mate out of a tight situation.

"Aboriginal families can get into arguments that go on and on and sometimes end up in a nasty fight," Paul would say, "but I could always depend on Charlie to help me out."

Paul signed up to play for the Balmain Tigers under 21's and that is how he came to be staying at Uncle Darryl's place in Sydney.

The night after Ralph and I visited Darryl, Paul came down to breakfast to see his uncle looking pale and nervous, like he had seen a ghost.

Darryl explained who had been at the house last night and that we had threatened him. Finally, Ralph left the police force.

Four months after the incident at Alexandria, my mother wrote a letter to the police, portions of which were reported in the Sydney Morning Herald:

'Mother Fears a Shoot Out'

The mother of the man police were chasing when they fired shots during Friday's Aboriginal sports carnival at Alexandria predicted a "serious tragedy" involving her son in a letter last March to the NSW Police Commissioner.

Mrs. Judith Quinlan, mother of Charles Quinlan, says she is still waiting for a reply.

Her letter warned Mr. Avery: "It would be an appalling tragedy if hot heads in your department were allowed to continue pushing......a young man into a blind alley."

In the letter, Mrs. Quinlan says she fears that her 26-year-old-son, nick-named Ned Kelly by North Coast police, will be forced to take up arms and kill a police officer in self-defence because of intense harassment."

"You [Mr. Avery] would do well to remind these fools what Ned Kelly did before they got to hanging him," she said.

Aborigines protesting the behaviour of police during Friday's attempted arrest will march on police headquarters tomorrow morning.'[1]

Other reports in the Sydney Morning Herald called for an investigation into police behaviour and showed up glaring differences between the testimony of the Aborigines and the police.

'Police Shots at Carnival: Inquiry Sought'

The NSW Aboriginal Legal Service (ASL) has called for a full inquiry into a incident in which plain-clothes police brandished pistols and a pump-action shot-gun at a large crowd of Aborigines during a sports carnival at Alexandria Park.

The ASL also wants criminal charges laid against the officers involved in the incident, which comes soon after the shooting of David Gundy.

Four witnesses have told the Herald that four shots were fired as police chased on foot an unarmed man wanted in connection with warrants. Women and children had screamed and dived for cover.

According to one witness, Mr. David Bell, who said it was lucky no-one in the crowd of about 2,000 people was killed, one of the shots was fired as the wanted man escaped in a truck in which there were young children.

Mr. Sol Bellear, a director of the Redfern Medical Service, who was at Alexandria Park at 4:30 p.m. on Friday said, "I was pulling kids out of the way of the police who were pointing guns. It was just bedlam. One of the guns, a little snub-nose revolver, wasn't even a police issue weapon."

A 14-year-old-girl, Shantelle Durgan, who recalled "jumping for cover" as a man armed with a pistol ran towards her, said, "I was so scared, I thought my brother had been shot."

Executive Chief Superintendent, Ken Chapman, acting commander of the south region said that the police rejected any suggestion that public safety had been endangered.

Only two shots had been fired, he said, and they had been to disperse a crowd of Aborigines who attacked two detectives who "feared for their safety."

Mr Chapman said that , "he completely endorsed" the actions of the two detectives who were among as many as eight officers from the South Region Crime Squad present at the scene.

He said an internal police investigation had been held and it was "completely satisfied" that only two shots were fired. The investigation did not interview any civilian witnesses.

According to Mr. Chapman, the incident was now being investigated by the Regional Investigative Group, which hoped to conclude its inquiries today.

Shane Phillips, of the Redfern Youth Action Group, which organised the carnival as part of National Aboriginal Day celebrations, said that at no stage did the officers identify themselves. "I was playing football when I saw this craze-faced man with a gun tackling a Koori bloke," said Mr. Phillips who is an officer into the Royal Commission into Black Deaths in Custody.

"We [football players] just ran in to separate them, and I grabbed this guy with the gun and wrestled with his hand, the hand that was holding the gun. The gun went off into the ground, and I kept shouting at him, "Stop shooting, stop shooting." He kept saying, "F... off, f... off."

Last night, the man wanted by the police, allegedly in connection with firearm offences, had not been caught.

The ALS chairman, Mr. Paul Coe said, " 31 statements had been taken from witnesses on Friday night." "They were all very similar," he said.'[2]

'People Dived for Cover, Witness Tells'

Mr Sol Bellear, director of the Redfern Aboriginal Medical Service, was a spectator during last Friday night's incident at Alexandria Park. He said he saw most of what 31 witnesses have alleged took place.

"I was standing around talking with other spectators and this Aboriginal bloke ran past me, and he was being chased by another bloke," Mr. Bellear said. "Then another guy, carrying a shoulder bag, ran up from Buckland Street end of the field and withdrew a pistol. He first fired a shot in the air. People were screaming and diving for cover. A woman shouted, 'It's a madman.'"

"On the field the game had stopped and the players were tackling the man with the gun. It was pointed at the ground and went off. Kids and other people were just running around screaming. Other officers...from different

directions.....were running in at this stage. There would be about three or four by now."

"One of the officers had a pump-action shotgun and he was moving its lever back and forward and pointing it at people. Wherever his eyes were the barrel was pointed. The aboriginal bloke had got free from the man when the man with the gun on his shoulder, fired another shot into the air."

"I was near a truck, pulling kids, some as young as four, out of the way and putting some of them in the truck. Two women were screaming blue murder and we thought they had been shot."

"The Aboriginal bloke just leapt into the truck and as he took off I heard another shot. Kids were jumping out of the back of the truck and some jumped into the cab. I heard the screech of tyres, the police were chasing the men out of the park."[3]

The next day The Sydney Morning Herald took up the story:

'He'll End Up Like Gundy'

Charlie Quinlan, the Aboriginal police were seeking when shots were fired at the sports on Friday, could become, "another David Gundy" according to an uncle.

"I know, I just know, that he is going to get shot," the uncle who asked not to be named, told the emotional protest rally in Redfern yesterday. "He'll end up like David Gundy."

[David Gundy was shot dead during a raid on his home in April by police looking for John Porter.]

Charlie Quinlan according to Aboriginal people in Redfern, has spent most of his life in the north of NSW. Late last year, he moved to Sydney and in Redfern, where he chose to live, Mr. Quinlan became "a good mate to have around."

He has some relatives in Sydney, some who told the meeting yesterday that they were scared police would search their homes in pursuit of Mr. Quinlan."[4]

'Police Warned 'No Guns At Sports'

Armed South Region Crime Squad officers were warned by colleagues not to use guns during Friday's crowded Aboriginal sports carnival at Alexandria, according to a liaison officer with the Redfern Police Aboriginal Liaison Unit.

Mr. Alan Johnson claims the officers were warned that the lives of civilians could be put at risk.

A major inquiry into the Alexandria Park incident has been announced by Assistant Police Commissioner Tony Lauer. He said, that, unlike some senior police, he would not be "completely satisfied" about what took place on Friday until the inquiry's outcome.

Mr. Lauer was responding to comments, reported in yesterday's Herald, by Executive Chief Superintendent Ken Chapman, who said he was satisfied with the actions of the police.

Yesterday a meeting of 150 Aborigines at Redfern decided to march on Police Headquarters on Thursday. The meeting, at Alexandria Park, also demanded an urgent meeting with the Premier and the absent Minister for Police, Mr. Pickering.

The NSW Aboriginal Legal Service collected more statements from witnesses of the incident and indicated that it would seek to lay criminal charges against the police involved.

According to Mr. Johnson, the Crime Squad's officers had "completely destroyed" a delicate operation in which the unarmed man they were seeking at the carnival was preparing to surrender to the Redfern Police. Mr. Johnson claimed Redfern police had known the man's whereabouts for six months.

"I am disgusted with the Crime Squad involved in Friday's incident," said Mr. Johnson, "I warned the Crime Squad men….that public safety – the lives of women and children – would be endangered if they tried to arrest the man with guns. Yet this warning was totally disregarded," he said, adding that his own warning had been echoed by other liaison officers.

Some witnesses of Friday's incident say four shots were fired as plain-clothes members of the Crime Squad tried to arrest the man, Charles Quinlan.

Women and Children, part of an estimated crowd of 2,000, dived for cover as the shots went off. A witness said a policeman armed with a pump-action shotgun pointed it at members of the crowd.

Mr. Johnson said, "Redfern Police knew that the man was willing to surrender himself....following sensitive discussions. More communication would have resulted in his surrender. Yet all this information was ignored. The liaison unit is just a token body. It is understandable that the Aboriginal community is outraged."

Mr Lauer said police had two warrants – neither for firearms offences – for Mr. Quinlan's arrest when they gathered at Alexandria Park in several unmarked police cars and a van.

One of the warrants related to a breach of bail entered into after an assault charge and the other alleged assault occasioning actual bodily harm.

According to Mr Lauer, only two shots were fired during the carnival incident, when Aborigines who had been playing football tackled an armed detective. He stated that department guidelines allow police to fire at an offender when he was fleeing.'[5]

The witnesses apparently did not realise that I had been shot, but my damaged finger and upper thigh scar are evidence that the bullet hit its mark. I had no intention of surrendering to the police; I knew they had a policy of 'shoot on sight' and 'don't ask questions'.

I again successfully evaded the police and made my way back to my cave living there peacefully for about six months.

......

1. Sydney Morning Herald *Mother fears a shootout*, Wednesday 19th July 1989, page 18, reporter Tony Hewett

2. Sydney Morning Herald, *Police shots at carnival: inquiry sought*, Monday 17th July 1989, page 2, reporter Tony Hewett

3. Sydney Morning Herald, *People dived for cover, witness tells*, Monday 17th July 1989, page 2, reporter Tony Hewett

4. Sydney Morning Herald, *'He'll end up like Gundy'*, Tuesday 18th July 1989, page 3 reporter Tony Hewett

5. Sydney Morning Herald, *Police warned 'no guns at sports'*, Tuesday 18th July 1989, page 3 reporters Tony Hewett and Lindsay Simpson

14

FRIEND OR FOE

From two years of age, my uncle, Darryl Wright, was raised by his grandmother at the Bellbrook Reserve. His grandmother, like Florence Nightingale, helped the sick and elderly. If anyone was struggling Mrs. Wright would take them in and feed them for a few days. It was not unusual for there to be twenty or more people under her roof.

Darryl often visited our family. Even after my dad, Ralph Quinlan, moved to Kundabung Darryl would bring his family to visit relatives at the Bellbrook Reserve. My father owned a horse named Whipstick. He won a lot of races on Whipstick. The course would be a lap of the Reserve. There were lots of horses in those days so horse races and flag racing, with socks on the poles for the flags, were held regularly. Plenty of dancing too, on the verandah of the school building, swaying to the beat of guitar, fiddle or accordion.

Darryl remembers Ralph as a hard worker. Ralph worked for the railways for years and was always looking for other work on holidays or weekends; mostly picking vegetables or cotton-chipping. Ralph injured his back while working in the railways. One day he was pushing a cart on the railway track when the cart flipped over and landed on him; but he never stopped working. Perhaps the accident put a strain on his heart.

Ralph Quinlan was well respected by his own people and by whites. An obituary written by Ralph's friend, Andrew Pacey and printed in the Macleay Argus, documented, 'He was a man held in great respect by his people and by the whites. Because of that, I must say it was one of the biggest funerals I have attended....the service was really touching. The hymns they sang had to be heard to be described. I can only say it was all beautiful. Apart for all this, I could not help noticing the entrance to the cemetery where railwaymen formed a guard of honour. These men were white and the trouble of doing this for one Aborigine is worth mentioning in my book.'[1] After dad died the family drifted apart. Mum eventually came to live on the Reserve and got involved with another man.

At the time my brother Ralph and I were getting into trouble Darryl was working for the police as an Aboriginal Liaison Officer negotiating issues both within Aboriginal communities and between the police and Aboriginals. Family feuding was out of control in the Mungindi community, on the New South Wales/Queensland border near Moree and police were powerless to stop the fighting. One of the community members was in hospital with an axe wound when Darryl was called in to negotiate peace.

"We'll hold the meeting in the court house," he said, "black fellas respect the court house. They won't fight there."

The police were sceptical but it worked. The rival factions calmed down long enough to talk about how the fighting started in the first place. Although there were some verbal arguments, in the end Darryl reminded them of the importance of family and how they could move on. After two hours they were crying and hugging each other.

The police asked Darryl to introduce them to people in the community.

"How do we go about it?" they asked.

"We just walk into the communities," Darryl answered. "If the people are sitting on the ground we sit with them; we do what they do."

There were never riots in Darryl's areas because he believed in communication and being seen in the community.

Darryl remembers some good men in the police force. Aboriginals showed respect for officers of high rank. Inspector Bruce Kerrison, the commander at Kempsey was a fair man. If there was a problem with junior officers Kerrison would move them on. Another policeman, Sergeant Thompson was stationed at Bellbrook when Darryl was growing up. The men on the mission would milk Thompson's cow. For his part, Thompson would take the mission kids fishing and teach them scouting.

Having Ralph and I as his nephews was a problem Darryl could have done without. Mum often rang Darryl, asking him to talk with the us boys. One day he received such a call.

"The boys are here," she said. "They're in trouble and they want to talk to you. They need you Darryl."

The police were also keen for Darryl to meet with us. They were hoping he could persuade us to give ourselves up. We, however, never had any intention of giving ourselves up. By the time Darryl arrived we had usually left.

Following the altercation with police at Coolongolook, Darryl was called in. Police had my skirt but that was all and I had escaped into the bush.

"You'll never find him now," Darryl told the officers, "he's a bushman like his father and grandfather."

Nevertheless the police asked Darryl to try tracking me. They gave him and another officer a horse each. Darryl soon found my trail, broken branches heading toward the river.

"You're wasting your time," he repeated, "Charlie's either gone upstream or downstream and could be anywhere now."

I saw him riding about that day but didn't show myself because a helicopter was flying overhead.

Police visiting Darryl the following day said, "You were right; Charlie jumped a train to Sydney. The trail's gone cold after that."

Darryl had many opportunities to talk to me and Ralph but could not bring himself to turn us in because we were family. The police encouraged him to persuade us to give ourselves up before we got shot. One day while attending a football match in Newcastle, a number of police arrived.

"We've got intelligence," they said. "Charlie's at the game. Have you seen him?"

Truthfully Darryl was able to say he had not.

"Maybe he's on the field," they suggested.

"No, he's not," Darryl replied. "Don't do anything; you'll likely start a riot."

Later Darryl was sitting on the ground, having a rest, when I walked up to him.

"Don't you know, the police have been here looking for you?" Darryl asked me. "You'd better move on quietly."

I had a grudge to settle and I was looking for a fight.

"Don't fight anyone, Charlie, you'll just make things worse. There are a lot of young people here and the police have guns."

Darryl was a good talker and was able to persuade me to leave.

Darryl claimed he was not at the park in Sydney on Aboriginal Day though I swear I saw him.

"I'm glad I wasn't there," Darryl says, "Charlie and Ralph could be pretty mean and Charlie had a bad temper at times."

Darryl will not talk much about the day Ralph and I threatened him but only says his fast talking got him out of a serious situation. Eventually he resigned; the job was just too hard. Aborigines wanted change but the police did not. He knew I was happy that he was not working with the police anymore.

Darryl tried to support me by attending some of my court cases and visiting me in the lock-up. He was pleased that Ralph was caught while he was out of the country so it could not be suggested he had had a part in the arrest but I was caught soon after he returned.

When I as well as Ralph and another cousin from Bellbrook were doing time in Long Bay Correctional Centre we asked Darryl to visit us. It was just him and us in a room by ourselves and Darryl was very frightened. He need not have been; we just wanted him to do some things for our families and my mother. Their relationship started to heal from that meeting.

The superintendent of the prison admitted to Darryl, "It's good having Charlie in this prison; we never have riots when he's here. Basically Charlie runs the prison. He's a big man here."

When I was released the police were observing me closely; they followed me around, watching my every move. Darryl objected, "Leave him alone, he's doing good."

"You're only saying that because you're his uncle."

"I'm not," Darryl insisted, "Charlie's trying to go straight and you're putting too much pressure on him."

One detective claimed he had a photo of me protecting a 13 million marijuana plantation and tried to pin the crime on me. Darryl knowing I had never taken drugs, not even cigarettes or alcohol, insisted the detective show him the photograph but the incriminating evidence was never presented.

Twelve months later the grandson of the same detective was jailed and hanged himself in his cell. The detective himself was charged for supplying marijuana. Darryl always said he was suspicious at the time because he thought the man was fat and lazy. Even his body language suggested he was not telling the truth.

My relatives either hated me or loved me. Some helped and supported me; others feared and disliked me. As the reward money for my capture increased some turned informer. I was safe while I stayed in our secret cave. I could have stayed there indefinitely but when my younger brother Ralph got into trouble I took a risk and headed for Sydney.

......

1. Macleay Argus, *A man says goodbye to a good friend*, Thursday, June 12, 1975

15

BROTHERS

I had two brothers, Darren three years younger than me and Ralph six years my junior. While some people hated me and Ralph they loved Darren. Peace-loving and honest, he grew up to be a good family man. When I embarked on my life of crime Darren took on the responsibility of the eldest son. While we were locked up he was father not only to his own children but to mine and Ralph's. I blame the heavy responsibility for driving my brother to drink. Darren tried to influence us even willing to give up the drink if Ralph and I would stop stealing but the we had chosen our path in life and were not willing to change. At times Darren felt unloved because we refused to involve him in our escapades but I realised Darren's temperament was not suited to our sometimes violent life of crime.

Ralph would not be denied. He idolised me and the wild life was his escape from an unhappy home. Ralph was the best fighter. He had no fear and would take on anyone but he unlike me would never shoot a man. Today his son Reynold is a professional fighter. I was a good fighter too but I always had a gun ready and if threatened was quick to use it.

Ralph and his mates committed crimes without me. He trusted too many people and some dobbed him in. Ralph ended up spending a lot more time in jail than me because there were so many witnesses. I was too smart to get involved with Ralph's mates. I did not trust them, but the police assumed we brothers were always working together. Often I would plan the crime without actually taking part. Consequently both of us were charged with crimes we did not commit.

One of my saddest memories was of all of us three brothers locked up at the same time, in the same cell at Grafton Prison. Darren was serving the small time, a month for drink driving. Ralph was in for a few months and I for a number of years. It broke my heart when Darren requested to do time in my place. The request was denied and he was the first to walk out the prison gates. More hugs and tears followed when Ralph was released. In our cell together we had a wonderful time, talking about our lives, reading the Bible together and discussing how we could change things. Nothing really changed in Darren's lifetime. Alcohol claimed his life at age 40. He had given up drinking a month earlier but it was too late.

Regardless of our path in life, we three brothers were fiercely protective of each other. When Darren was bashed in Kempsey at the Macleay Hotel, Ralph and I went on a rampage of retribution. Ten aboriginal men were involved in the assault and one by one Ralph and I tracked them down and gave them a beating. The town was in fear as we drove past the perpetrators homes wildly shooting. The whole affair put the police back on our trail.

When I was finally released from Long Bay Jail for the last time Ralph was still a prisoner. On Ralph's release I employed him in my construction business. Ralph had only been out of jail for a week when I and a workmate had our construction business in Sydney. I owned a sporty orange car at the time and Ralph pleaded with me to leave him the car for the weekend. I was very reluctant not only because I didn't like lending my car but in the past Ralph was never out of jail long before committing another crime.

That weekend the Bowling Club at South West Rocks was robbed and Ralph was arrested in Kempsey at the wheel of the orange vehicle. He served time in prison for armed robbery. I wish I hadn't loaned Ralph my car. The car was like a neon light. At the same time Ralph insisted he was innocent of the crime. Ralph was arrested less than an hour after the incident at South West Rocks started. There is no way he could have been at South West Rocks, committed the crime and been back in Kempsey at the time he was arrested. I believe Ralph was convicted because of his past record and association with others who actually committed the offence.

Ralph was transferred to the jail at Windsor. He completed the Anger Management Course required for parole and was due for release in about a month. Ralph has earned his own reputation in jail. A violent inmate was locked in a dry cell threatening to kill screws. Ralph claimed if they would transfer the man to his cell he'd settle him down.

The 'big boss' from the jail came to see Ralph.

"He won't muck up if you put him with me."

Permission was denied but after another two men were attacked, prison officers relented and put the prisoner with Ralph.

"Now, you're here," Ralph said, "there's conditions. You've got to be quiet, don't do anything."

The once violent inmate became peaceful; all he wanted to do was to be with Ralph. He noticed Ralph reading his Bible and now he's reading the Bible too. The fear is that Ralph is too valuable to be released from jail.

Police officers from Port Macquarie asked Ralph if he would testify against a former accomplice whom they had recently arrested. Ralph refused so they threatened to charge him with the crime, a robbery committed some years ago. Ralph's parole is now in jeopardy. I think it's all a ploy to keep Ralph in jail and make him serve his full term. Ralph knows too much about corruption in the police force and he could make trouble for some officers once he's free. The robbery charge is unlikely to stick but it will delay Ralph's release. It's discouraging for Ralph. He's worked hard for early release and now it's not likely to happen.

16

———————

CAPTURE

By November 1989 both I and my brother Ralph were notorious wanted men.

'Police believe that two Aboriginal brothers wanted for various stealing, violence and weapons offences may be hiding out in the Redfern area. Ralph Reynold Quinlan, 21 and Charles Frederick Quinlan, 27, are probably armed and dangerous, police said. Ralph Quinlan is 176 cm tall and solid, with dark hair and brown eyes. He has a tattoo of a foreign word on his left shoulder blade, the letter R on his right shoulder and a 6 cm scar on the lower right leg.'[1]

While I was living comfortably in my cave, Ralph had got himself into trouble. Detective Roger Rogerson had his own crew; his gang did the robberies and he looked after them. Ralph was stepping over the boundary, committing robberies on Rogerson's turf. I was alerted to Ralph's danger by his friend Dennis.

Dennis used to pay me to accompany him to horse races. Dennis carried large amounts of cash on him, up to $100,000. I was paid $10,000 a night to protect Dennis. Dennis was a gambler. He was involved in fixing bets but because of his connections with police he never got in trouble.

The police had told Dennis to tell the 'big fella' to warn his brother to get off their turf. The message was 'do your robberies elsewhere and we won't arrest you.' So I left the cave and found Ralph in Sydney. I passed on the warning but Ralph was too confident and continued committing robberies wherever he wanted. By this time there was a big reward for information leading to my and Ralph's capture. In the past family members had helped me and others were too scared to help the police. But one hundred and fifty grand was a lot of money. My plan was to grab Ralph and bring him back to the cave but Ralph got caught.

I was spending the night in Sydney with my daughter Mandy. My guns were under my pillow as usual.

Mandy had gone to the shops down the road but when she returned she told me, "Daddy, Daddy, there is lot a men on the corner slapping each other."

I knew at once this was Tactical Response Men psyching themselves up for a raid. I ran out the back of the house, forgetting my guns, but the place was already surrounded.

"Mr. Quinlan, lie down, lie down, we have you surrounded," ordered a voice over a loudspeaker. "Lie down, we'll count to three then shoot."

Mandy ran out, "Please Daddy, lie down."

She had been around both times I had been shot in the past and now she was in the middle of the fray again.

"One... two...... three...!"

No-one fired.

Again they counted but I would not drop. At that point a helicopter hovered overhead and four men abseiled out right onto me wrestling me to the ground before gassing and handcuffing me. I suppose I should have been happy not to have been shot. I was escorted to the CBD in an escape-proof van.

Liberal opposition leader Nick Greiner came into power in 1988. I always reckoned I helped Nick become Premier of New South Wales. Nick Greiner built a powerful election platform, underpinned by harsh campaign rhetoric on significant anti-corruption and criminal justice reforms.

A picture of the capture of notorious criminal Charlie Quinlan, who had evaded the police net for so long, was used in Greiner's extensive television advertising during the campaign. Once in power Greiner engineered a rush of legislation, thirty-seven laws in four months.

The late 80's New Right opened an assault on social movements; beginning with Aborigines and the gay and lesbian community, followed by public housing, education and health cuts. Greiner is infamous for making goals more barbaric and bringing in a phalanx of anti-union laws. Ironically the coalition's ICAC (Independent Commission Against Corruption) was the cause of the Premier's resignation in 1992. With the aid of detailed information from a couple of well-known Sydney "crims" the commission that brought about Nick Greiner's departure from state politics has turned its attention to corruption within the New South Wales' police force.[2]

In jail my reputation went before me and I worked hard to keep up the image. In the exercise yard I lifted weights and worked out to keep in shape. Consequently I was the undisputed boss of the Aboriginal inmates.

The picture on the next page is of myself and other inmates in Long Bay Jail. I'm the one in the middle, the 'boss' man. My brother, Ralph, flexing his muscles is second from the right.

Charlie in his prime

Keeping in shape was critical for my safety

......

1. Sydney Morning Herald, *Crime stoppers*, Thursday November 30 1989, page 17

2. www.greenleft.org.au/1992/82/1983 sighted 05.02.2009

17

RIOTS

Australian prisons, as in other countries, have a chequered history. In the early days of transportation convicts were housed in tents, working part of the day for the government and part of the day privately to pay their rent. Although prisons were built to house the most intractable convicts and floggings were common, many prisoners had opportunity to work for assigned masters in 'service' to see out their sentence.

In 1835 a parliamentary committee recommended the building of new prisons at Sydney and Parramatta. It was proposed that prisoners be physically isolated from one another and banned from communicating with each other. An 1849 inquiry into the administration of Darlinghurst Gaol found "debauchery, drunkenness and irregularity of every kind"[1] and the officers involved were dismissed.

In 1878 allegations of cruelty at Berrima Jail led to a royal commission. It recommended that gagging and the practice of 'spread-eagling' (where prisoners are chained to a wall), be abolished.

Over the next century certain reforms were introduced; the imprisonment of children was halted as was the placement of mentally disturbed people in prisons. A separate prison for women was constructed at Long Bay and leg-ironing of prisoners in transit was stopped. By 1925 bathing was allowed each working day instead of twice weekly. Calling at half-hourly intervals by night guards was abandoned and lights in cells were permitted. Prisoners serving two or more years were allowed writing materials in their cells.[2]

In the face of these reforms, conditions in Grafton Jail during my first internment turned back the pages of history. I was beaten frequently and was only permitted two showers per week. Increasing tensions in the state's prisons as well as a number of serious assaults on prison officers led to Grafton Jail being used to house the most intractable prisoners. The penal methods at Grafton over the next thirty-three years are described as a 'regime of terror', 'brutal, savage and some-times sadistic'. This period is labelled as 'one of the most sordid and shameful episodes in NSW penal history'. "It became abundantly clear during the Commission's hearings that the arduous duties required of [Grafton's prison] officers largely consisted of inflicting brutal, savage, and sometimes sadistic physical violence on the hapless group of intractables who were sent to Grafton."[3]

A 1946 report on prison reform found overcrowding at Long Bay. It recommended that sewerage replace pan systems in major jails and prisoners should have two more hours each day out of their cells. In 1970 a major riot erupted at the 19th century Bathurst Jail. Prisoners spent eighteen hours a day in their cells and no glass in the windows meant bedding was often soaked by rain. Sewerage created health problems as lavatories regularly overflowed and cisterns jammed.

After the riot, some prison officers participated in a systematic flogging of prisoners. In February 1974 there was a second, larger riot at Bathurst Gaol. Petrol bombs were thrown about the prison complex and officers fired on inmates. The jail was gutted by fire and cost $10 million to rebuild.

Katingal Gaol at the Long Bay complex was opened in 1975. It was designed exclusively for six categories of violent prisoners, including top protection cases. The special cells were devoid of natural light, all doors were electronically operated, food was passed through the hatch and the prisoners were allowed no direct contact with prison officers.

Prisoners were denied privileges or programs available to other inmates.

Recommendations by the 1976 Royal Commission set up to investigate the Bathurst Prison riots and headed by Justice Nagel resulted in the closure of Katingal after just three years of operation. The report also found that the NSW Department of Corrective Services and ministers of both major parties had unofficially sanctioned the systematic brutalisation of prisoners at Grafton Gaol.

During my internment at Long Bay Correctional Centre drugs were available to anyone with money and corruption was rampant. You could get out of prison if you had enough money. In 1983 allegations surfaced that the NSW Minister for Corrective Services, Rex Jackson, had accepted payments in return for granting early release to certain prisoners. In 1987 Jackson was convicted of conspiracy in relation to the early licence release scheme. A 1985 task force found 78 per cent of women in jail were addicted to alcohol or drugs, especially heroin.[4]

A 1999 inquiry by the Independent Commission Against Corruption (ICAC) into Corrective Services found officers developed improper relationships with inmates by accepting bribes to tamper with prison documents.

In 1990 Geoffrey Pearce, a 22-year-old probationary prison officer at Long Bay Gaol was stabbed by an inmate with a syringe containing HIV-infected blood. Following the shock of this news Minister Yabsley, the Minister for Corrective Services, implemented a major campaign to remove prisoners' personal property from prison cells. The result of the removal of personal effects was riots and even an investigation by Amnesty International.[5] The officer subsequently tested positive to the virus and in 1997 he died from an AIDS-related illness.

In Eileen Balfry's paper, "*The Changing Boundaries: What Place Community Organisation in Change and Reforms of the Criminal Justice System*" she states her paper has as its background, the devastation wrought upon the criminal justice system in the state of NSW between 1988 and 1991. The ministry at that time, headed by Mr Michael Yabsley, increased the prison population by 48 per cent, dismantled prison welfare services, cut funds to post-release services and lengthened sentences by 19 % (due to the so-called "truth-in-sentencing" legislation).[6]

I was in the Long Bay Correctional Centre when a riot broke out in that facility. Arthur Schubert was the governor at the time. In earlier days I remember him as hard man. As the head of the Classification Board Schubert determined where a prisoner would be interned.

I had stood in front of him when he said, "You've got two choices of where you'll be interned, Grafton or Grafton."

"I'll take Grafton." I smugly replied.

Prisoners would beg not to go to Grafton such was the goal's brutal reputation. However over time both Schubert and I have changed and now we're friends.

I was lying in my cell when I first heard the fracas. Around five hundred inmates were milling around in the holding yard. Ross, a big bloke, was standing on the table, gesturing and shouting, urging the prisoners to burn the jail to the ground.

"What's happening?" I asked.

"Don't you know? Prisoners are rioting all over the state? A bunch of screws have locked themselves up in room 12 at the Metropolitan Remand Centre. We're going to get fuel and oil from the maintenance room and torch this dump!"

In the perimeter outside the prison wall I could see a fleet of police cars and the infamous riot squad.

"Charlie, be with us, give the okay and this place will go up!"

I tried 'to calm the mob down, "Don't do anything 'til I come back. I'm going to see the governor first."

I got permission to see Mr. Schubert. I usually enjoyed a visit to the governor; Schubert would serve me milo, cake and biscuits while we discussed prisoners' issues. This time Schubert's face was grave.

"Charlie, we've been friends for a long time, all I want from you is to let the officers out of the wing, then lock yourself in your cell so nothing happens to you."

"Look Mr. Schubert, I've come to talk with you, but first I need to go the toilet." I replied.

Schubert was nonplussed, "Well.., you know where it is."

I did not need the toilet but I did need a quiet place. I had no idea how to stop the riot.

Talking with my eyes open, looking at my hands, I spoke to God, "God, thank you for these hands, thank you that I'm alive because I know I shouldn't be. I'm sorry for what I've done in my life. You know our situation here".

I prayed for the prisoners; I prayed for the governor. "Help me please."

As I walked back to the governor's office I still didn't know what to do but I felt at peace. As I walked a plan formed in my mind.

As I sat down Schubert asked, "What happened to you, you look different?"

"Just washed me face," I lied.

"Look Mr. Schubert, I'm going to ask you to trust me, I can assure you this jail will not riot. I'll go back and let the officers out on one condition. We must come to an agreement - no make that three agreements."

"You sure you don't want four," Schubert grimaced.

"First demand is you give me access to the maintenance area."

The two officers next to Schubert interrupted, "What! That's where the gas and oil is kept."

"I know," said Schubert, "What else?"

"Second demand is for inmates to get back their phone and visitation rights. Third demand is for a green light to the kitchen when the boys are back in their cells. After this do you think I could come home with you?"

Schubert laughed, "After this who knows that you might, but seriously I'll agree to your demands but I can't throw away the key. I'll see you about the fourth demand when this is all over."

We shook hands and I returned to find my brother Ralph.

Ralph was all fired up; he was young and thought that rioting would be a grand lark. We followed the prison wardens to the maintenance area, unlocked the room and selected two sledgehammers.

Back in the holding yard, Ross was still whipping up the prisoners into a frenzy. I stood on another table. The prisoners respected me. I knew they would listen to me.

"Hands up anyone who's been in a riot before?"

About fifty or sixty hands went up, mostly older men.

"Move over to this side," I instructed. "All you older men, who've been in prison for ages, move over too."

"What yer doing Charlie? This is a waste of time," someone shouted.

"I'm just giving these men a choice," I replied. "Who 'ere still has trials waiting, who's got outstanding courts - stand over 'ere."

I glanced at a prisoner, "When's yours, buddy,"

"Next month," the man replied.

"How's it lookin'?"

"Good."

"Well, if you're in a riot you'll get another ten years."

By this time well over three hundred men had joined my side.

"Who wants visits, see yer wives and kids? Who wants phone calls?"

Men drifted across. Now only about twenty men were left in the group who wanted to riot and burn.

"Let me tell you about a riot," I continued. "You ever been in a riot, Ross?"

"No, but I want to be in one!" Ross was belligerent. "What are the sledgehammers for?"

"Oh them, there're to knock off the door hinges. When you riot, the riot squad chase yer to your cell, lock yer up, gas yer and bash yer."

"Ross you're my brother. Ralph, hand him a sledgehammer. These blokes don't have go through that but Ross and me, we'll go and bust the hinges. I've been in riots; you get shot with rubber bullets, sometimes real ones if the screws want to get rid of yer. Ross and I will go and riot, the rest of yer go back to your cells."

The older men were nodding their heads and the men started heading for their cells. In the end only Ralph, me and Ross were left and Ross reluctantly returned to his cell. I asked for some officers to accompany me to room 12. The trapped officers were not willing to come out. They knew only too well that grudges would be settled if they were to fall into the hands of the prisoners. Only after talking to the governor himself did they come out and then they could not stop shaking my hand.

"Thank you, thank you."

Ralph and I went to the kitchen and loaded trolleys with food.

"We need a big feed," I told Ralph.

Biscuits, cream, butter, honey and jam, anything we could find, was piled high onto the trolleys and wheeled around the cells to the prisoners.

"When can we make the phone calls?"

"Soon, soon," I replied.

The governor came and sat with me in my cell.

"Mate, I'm really happy, I've never seen anything like this before. What's your fourth demand? You know I can't release you."

"We got a Catholic priest coming in here and some pastors from other denominations but my brother and I, we're Seventh-day Adventists. The Catholic priest has stopped our pastor from visiting. My fourth demand is you to open the chapel on Friday nights for our pastors to meet with us and for any Seventh-day Adventists who don't want to work on the Sabbath to have access to their cells."

"There's one more thing, I've a young lady I want to marry and I'm real sick of this prison tucker."

The officers ordered pizza and Kentucky fried for Ralph and me. Friday night the chapel was packed. Pastor Frank Saunders and Pastor George Quinlan came to minister to the prisoners. On November 24th 1992, Arthur Schubert was an honoured guest at my and Luana's wedding at Long Bay Jail.

History proves allegations of brutality during and after riots were true. In reporter Chris Master's interview with Professor David Brown Read of the University of New South Wales, Read testifies concerning the 1970 Bathurst riot; "The 1970 riot was a peaceful protest in which prisoners had agreed to go back to their cells, and they were then systematically flogged cell by cell - assaulted by very heavy prisoner officers, led by the superintendent. Prisoners gave very, very graphic accounts to the Royal Commission of hearing the cries as they came nearer and nearer, cell by cell, and you knew what they could expect. Then the aftermath of that of course was to deny that it had happened and maintain that denial over fairly implausibly a long period of time."

"It wasn't really until Nagle reported in 1978 that it laid that denial to rest and basically upheld the accounts of the prisoners of what happened in that time. So it's the routine violence, brutality in this case, actually led by the superintendent of the prison and then the significant cover-up and the ability to avoid any responsibility or accountability in relation to that unlawful behaviour."

"Then obviously the same sore was festering away also in Bathurst leading, in part, to the more major full scale riot in '74 that led to the burning down of half the gaol and then similarly reprisal bashings in the form of the gauntlet, both at Bathurst as prisoners were rounded up, and then later on another gauntlet at Long Bay, when prisoners were transferred there. Exactly the same pattern. The attempt at both a departmental and a political cover up, a denial this had happened and reaching into the levels of the government and through to the attorney general. An attempt to denigrate the prisoners, to say that they were unreliable, who would believe these people because they were convicted criminals, and then an attempt to stifle any inquiry by charging those prisoners with a series of offences, which a number of them were ultimately convicted and some were served longer gaol terms. And then finally leading to the calling of the Royal Commission as it was impossible to sustain those denials. So we have pretty unchecked brutality and the feeling you can get away with it."

In response to Master's question whether prisoners were fired upon indiscriminately, Read relied, "Yes, people were fired at. In some of the bashings in both riots, some officers refused to take part, but yes, it was a pretty shambolic response. There wasn't an organised kind of riot squad, individual officers were firing. People were shot. One prisoner was rendered a paraplegic as a result of firearm injuries."

Read was asked what he thought the explanation could be for the doubling of imprisonment rates across Australia in the '80s and '90s. He replied, "It's hard to say exactly. There's probably a range of features. We have things feeding into it, like the tighter restrictions on bail. An increasing proportion of that population are on remand. Currently remands are running between 20 and 25 per cent. That means between a fifth and a quarter of prisoners in gaol have not yet been convicted. That is, at the moment they're notionally innocent. Increased policing, increased level of penalties - the legislature setting higher penalties and courts giving out higher penalties. An increasing proportion of those prisoners will be a disproportionate increase in relation to women and indigenous prisoners, And public and political sentiment, a populist sort of attack on criminals that's carried out in sections of the media and picked up in a popular political way, led I think in the mid-80s by people like Michael Yabsley, and that proved to be very politically popular."[7]

......

1. http://www.policensw.com/info/history/darlgaol.html   *The   Old Darlinghurst Goal*

2. www.abc.net.au/4corners/content/2005/20050711_supermax/prison-chronology.htm *Chronology - A History of Australian Prison Reform*

3. www.abc.net.au/4corners/content/2005/20050711_supermax/prison-chronology.htm *Chronology - A History of Australian Prison Reform*

4. www.abc.net.au/4corners/content/2005/20050711_supermax/prison-chronology.htm *Chronology - A History of Australian Prison Reform*

5. http://www.aic.gov.au/publications/proceedings/04/kirby.pdf *WHO Global Commission, AIDS*

Recommendations and Prisons in Australia, Michael Kirby

6. *The Changing Boundaries: What Place Community Organisation in Change and Reforms of the Criminal Justice System*, page 1, Eileen Balfry

7. www.abc.net.au/4corners/content/2005/s1497246.htm 07/112005 *Interview - Professor David Brown Read an edited transcript of Chris Masters' discussion with Professor David Brown, NSW University, on Australian prison reform*, reporter Chris Masters

18

CHANGE

While in the Long Bay Correctional Centre, I, like other inmates awaiting parole was required to participate in an Anger Management Course. Satisfactory completion of the course was one of the requirements before parole would be considered. About thirty men would sit around in a circle while the psychologist took notes.

A discussion would take place, sometimes becoming violent.

A typical question directed at an inmate would be, "What are you in for?"

"Murder," was the reply.

"You murdered that old lady, how would you like it if she was your grandmother?"

The inmate in the 'hot seat' would be sweating it out, anger boiling until he started throwing punches.

The course took twelve months and prisoners had to demonstrate they could control their anger before being released. If a prisoner did not pass the course he would be placed in segregation and have to repeat the course.

The previous day I had been in the 'hot seat'. Today was Sunday, visitor's day, and my mother, my sister Lena and baby Charlie Junior were there.

I remember holding my son and thinking to myself, "I've got to get out; I don't need this anymore, got to do the right thing by my kids."

I thanked God for my namesake, who was now about six months old, with eyes alert. As I felt his little hands the thought occurred to me that the Anger Management Course was really helping me. I did not want to let Charlie go but soon the visit ended.

Later I rang home and spoke to Lena.

"Put on Mum, sis," I said. "I had a good visit today mum. I love my son, I know I've got to stop going to jail. You were right. The kids will come to me in the end."

"Don't you worry Charlie," mum replied, "your boy's in good hands. You'll see him when you get out."

I had dozed off in my cell, but woke about one or two in the morning. I'd had a dream.

I saw my daughter Mandy on one side of me and baby Charlie on the other saying, "Wake up! Wake up!"

I woke up in a cold sweat wondering what the dream could mean. In the next anger management session I mentioned the dream.

Immediately the pressure was on, "You've been on the drugs, Charlie."

"No mate, never taken drugs," I responded.

An officer interrupted the session, "Charlie, the welfare officer wants to see you."

In the welfare officer's room the officer was very quiet, "Sit down Charlie, we need to talk. I've some bad news."

My mum, I thought, my heart racing.

"Your son," the officer continued. "He was rushed off to the hospital this morning; but I'm sorry he was dead on arrival."

I couldn't think; I felt my heart was being ripped out of his chest. I was gnashing my teeth and banging the table with my fists, feeling my life completely crushed.

In consideration of the tragedy my mum was allowed to visit me the next day. I wanted to sign out of the course but mum talked me into continuing.

Lying alone in my cell I prayed, "There's nothing for me God, please help me, I'm in a mess."

As I prayed a light shone through the window directly onto my bedside table where my Bible lay. The Bible had gathered a lot of dust. I blew off the dust and flicked through the pages. I read a verse in the book of Job, *"Can the papyrus grow up without a marsh, can the reeds flourish without water? While it is yet green and not cut down, so are the paths of all that forget God......... behold this is the joy of His way, and out of the earth others will grow. Behold God will not cast away the blameless, nor will He uphold the evildoers. He will yet fill your mouth with laughing and your lips with rejoicing."* [1]

I remembered the story of Job whose seven sons and three daughters had been killed when a strong wind had brought down their house on them. Later they were replaced by the birth of another seven sons and three daughters and God had blessed Job. All Job's wealth had been taken from him but later God made him wealthier than he had been before. I was encouraged to believe God had not deserted me.

The prophecy was to be realised in the birth of 'Charles Frederick Tyrone Samson Lorenzo Quinlan' to my wife, Luana. Another son, with Eileen, was born three weeks later. Eileen didn't want another boy after her baby, Charles Dylan Rees Quinlan, had died, so one day she came up to me at a football match and thrust baby Edward into my arms. The boy was in a poor state, his nappy and singlet so soiled they stuck to his thin body. So Edward became a member of my and

Luana's family. One by one the children did return to me just as my mother had predicted.

......

1. Job 8:11-13, 19-21

19

DEATHS IN CUSTODY

While in Long Bay Correctional Centre I became a founding member of the Juvenile Aid Group (JAG) set up by the prisoners and a social worker. JAG was an organisation of lifers and experienced men to help young offenders. These men would talk to the youngsters as soon as they arrived, to help them understand the prison system. They taught them how to contact their parents, how to complete forms for access and visits as well as helping them with any other problems they had. Many young men were scared so it was reassuring to know that some experienced men would be looking after them.

I talked to one young Aboriginal man. The prisoner had just turned eighteen and was agitated, crying at night, worried about his twin brother who was being held in the Metropolitan Remand Centre. Both brothers were in jail for serious crimes; armed robbery and murder. His outside contact was a grandmother and he didn't want her to know they were in prison.

"Don't tell my grandmother, she'll end up in hospital. My brother is on the other side (the MRC). He's got nothing to do with this. They arrested him first but he's innocent so I confessed. The coppers.....they don't believe me. I want my brother in the cell with me."

"I'll try," I promised.

I approached the duty officer. "This boy's upset; he needs his brother in his cell with him."

The transfer was refused on the grounds that the boy was classified as a high profile prisoner.

I rang the governor, Mr. Schubert, who replied, "Whatever the officer on duty decides, that's how it will be. That's the system."

"At least take out his shoelaces, I'm afraid for this boy," I continued to plead with the duty officer right up to the time they were put in their cells for the night.

In the end the best he could do was give the boy a jug and a toaster as a simple caring gesture.

In the morning I heard people singing out. Looking out his cell window I saw officers outside the young man's cell. During the night the boy had hung himself from his cell window. The note he left behind asked his brother to forgive him, said he was sorry to his grandmother and swore that his brother was innocent of the crime. I gave evidence at the inquest as I was one of the last to see the young man alive but my evidence was ignored. Perhaps it might have been better if I had not given evidence. Due to my reputation and criminal history the court did not believe me. The innocent twin was convicted of the crimes and is serving his sentence.

I have my own opinions about Aboriginal deaths in custody. While I agree that some are suicide, others I believe are the result of police covering up their own brutality, while yet others are accidental. When a young man attempts to hang himself he may not mean to commit suicide but pressure on a nerve in the neck causes the person to pass out and a death may accidentally occur.

In 1981, Eddie Murray, the brother of one of my girlfriends, Eileen Murray, was out drinking with male family members in their home town of Wee Waa in north-west New South Wales. Eddie was celebrating his up-coming selection for a tour of New Zealand with the

Aboriginal All Blacks but got so drunk he was asked to leave the local pub. Police locked him up in the station's cell, using their 'discretion' under the Intoxicated Persons Act (1979).

The police could have taken him home, but instead kept him in custody.

Eddie was heard to cry out from his cell, "Why do you always pick on me? Why don't you pick on the white people?"

After being in custody only ninety minutes, Eddie was found hanged in his cell. His blood alcohol level at the time of his death was 0.3. Police claimed Eddie suicided. Before a police photographer arrived to take pictures of Eddie, his body had been removed from the cell in which he died. The next day, his clothes were missing.

When the Coroner looked into the matter, he found instances of unreliability in the evidence offered by police to the court. When the coroner looked into the matter, he returned an open verdict, stating "Death at the hand of person or persons unknown"... He also said there was no evidence that Murray took his own life.[1]

By the time Lloyd Boney died at Brewarrina in 1987, the sixteenth death that year, Prime Minister, Bob Hawke, was prepared to listen to the Committee to Defend Black Rights. The Royal Commission into Aboriginal Deaths in Custody, appointed in 1987, then inquired into 99 deaths between January 1980 and April 1991, concluding with 339 recommendations in five volumes. The commission was critical of police evidence in the Eddie Murray case but concluded there was no basis for a finding of police culpability in what was assumed to be suicide.

The Murray family pushed for a further investigation into Eddie's death. They were at the forefront of the call for a Royal Commission of Inquiry into Aboriginal deaths in custody. When the Royal Commission inquired into Eddie's death, more examples of police inconsistencies were exposed. The New South Wales Attorney General at that time, Terry Sheahan, promised the Murray family that the New South

Wales government would fully investigate any new evidence in the case.

In 1997 Eddie's body was exhumed and it was found that he had suffered a fractured breastbone, which was probably caused by one or more blows to his chest. This discovery led to further questions about whether he could have hanged himself. In August 2000 the then Minister for Police, Paul Whelan, referred the case to the New South Wales Police Integrity Commission (PIC).

In the subsequent inquiry, Professor Nikolai Bogduk, Professor of Anatomy and Musculoskeletal Medicine testified, "An individual with a fractured sternum would have their chest pain strongly aggravated by movements such as lifting the arms above the head to hold or pull objects. What we take for granted when reaching up, in terms of being able to balance the upper limb as we reach up or out, would be impaired."[2]

The Police Integrity Commission conducted what it termed a preliminary investigation into Eddie's case that lasted almost as long as the duration of the entire Royal Commission of Inquiry into Aboriginal Deaths in Custody, examining a total of 99 deaths. Within three years the Police Integrity Commission examined only nine documents, procured only four more documents, and spoke to eleven people. At the conclusion of this period, the PIC did not offer the New South Wales parliament a report into its so-called 'investigation'. Using its secrecy provisions, a limited account of its activities was offered to the Murray family's legal advisers.

Eddie's parents, Arthur and Leila Murray, embarked on a search for truth and fought for over twenty years to have the death of their son properly investigated. Subsequently in the book, *Eddie's Country*, Simon Luckhurst delved deeply into the official inquiries carried out since Eddie's death. He chronicled the Murray family's experience with the Royal Commission into Aboriginal Deaths in Custody. Despite the findings of the commissions Eddie's father in no way accepts that his son took his own life.

In much of black Australia, suicide is no longer something alien, an act for which there is no word in any Aboriginal language. The human act of self-inflicted, self-intentional cessation of life has now become a pattern. Outside of custody Aboriginals enjoy suicide rate that was among the lowest in the world but now has become among the world's highest in a little more than twenty-five years.

In a Senate speech on the 6th of September, 2000 Koori Democrats Senator, Aden Ridgeway, expressed his disappointment at the lack of commitment to addressing the question of deaths in custody. Senator Ridgeway said before the royal commission, "About 12% of all prison deaths were of Indigenous people, but in the last decade that figure has risen to 18%. Sadly the national picture for 1999 is in keeping with the 20-year trend to date. Indigenous people, who comprise just over 2% of our national population, made up 22% of all deaths in custody."[3]

......

1.   www.parliament.nsw.gov.au/prod/parlment/HansArt.nsf/V3Key/LC20040225047 *Death of Mr. Eddie Murray Enquiry*

2. www.abc.net.au/7.30/stories/s69095.htm *Family calls for Eddie Murray case to be reopened*, transcript 26/11/1999

3.   www.faira.org.au/lrq/archives/200009/stories/custody_deaths_story.html *Who's To Blame*, September 2000

20

SAXON'S ESCAPE

I never tried to escape from prison. I know what it was like to be on the run and hunted like an animal so I was prepared to serve my time, working to get early parole. That did not mean I wouldn't help others escape. When I arrived at Long Bay Jail a tunnel had already been started, the boys getting their idea from the war film, *The Great Escape*. It took four years to complete as men came and went taking their turns at digging.

The entrance to the tunnel was under the education room in the exercise yard. The exercise yard was a big area, concreted now but during the tunnel episode it was grassed. The men would dig using their enamel eating bowls and cups, hiding the dirt in their pockets and trouser bottoms. In the yard they would casually sit on the ground or lie down for a rest surreptitiously scattering the dirt on the grass. The tunnel was perhaps 10 metres long, as high as man with just enough width to walk down. A deeper section was dug under the wall extending a metre or more under the ground and that tunnel finished a short distance outside the perimeter.

I was on shift the day a man could poke his finger through the grass outside the wall. The escape for hundreds of prisoners was planned for the following night. It was amazing that no-one squealed, considering the number of prisoners involved, but turning informer wasn't worth your life. Stabbings were all too common in jail. The authorities did try at times to place informers in the prison but they didn't last long. The inmates had a reception committee to meet all new prisoners.

Questions were asked, "This yer first time? How long's yer sentence? Who do yer know?"

It was soon known who might be working for the police and they would be removed.

On the day of the escape the prisoners lined up for phone calls as usual.

All phone calls were monitored and a few comments alarmed the listening officers, "I'll see you tonight."

"I'll be home soon."

Some of these callers were serving long sentences. The jail was locked down and sniffer dogs brought in. The dogs found the tunnel. Some of the more dangerous criminals were moved but a wall of silence ensured no-one was convicted of anything.

On 26 January 1990, Ian Hall Saxon, an infamous rock band promoter turned drug baron, was arrested and charged with a number of matters arising out of his involvement in the importation of cannabis resin into Australia. He was refused bail and held in the Metropolitan Remand Centre (MRC) in the Long Bay complex. At the time of his arrest $5.5 million in cash, together with a quantity of Kruger rands, gold bars and hashish were found in a Coogee garage rented by Saxon's associates.

Realising he faced a lengthy prison sentence, Saxon was determined to escape. Prior to the commencement of his committal proceedings in September 1990, Saxon was suspected of planning an escape attempt. Consequently prison authorities put him on a 'short lease' for a couple of years.

By late 1992, Saxon circumstances had improved. He had achieved a position in the MRC whereby he had two jobs. He worked as a clerk with the Assistant Superintendent of Industries' office (ASI) and also in the prison library.

While on remand in March 1993 Saxon staged a daring escape. A number of theories were put forth about how Saxon escaped. The popular belief was that Ian Saxon left the jail in the store's delivery van. Saxon himself gave another version. In 1996 he was tracked down in California and extradited to Australia where he was sentenced to twenty-four years imprisonment. On being extradited back to Australia, Saxon was charged with escaping from lawful custody. He pleaded not guilty and on 27 September 1995 was committed for trial on that charge.

On 4 February 1997, Saxon gave evidence under oath at a private hearing of the Commission which was held at Maitland for security reasons. He told the Commission that on the evening of the first of March 1993 he had fallen asleep in his cell in 12 Wing dressed in a tee-shirt and track pants. Some time later he was wakened by two figures entering his room. These figures were dressed in uniforms and black boots similar to those worn by members of the Malabar Emergency Unit (MEU). Saxon claimed he lost consciousness believing he had been sedated by these persons. Taken to a house in Newton he later escaped from the room by climbing out of a window onto the roof of an outhouse below.

It was all a wild fabrication. Later he changed his story to more or less correspond with the testimony of three inmates, unidentified in the Commissions proceedings. These three inmates who gave evidence implicated themselves in the escape of Saxon from lawful custody but under section 38 of the ICAC Act their evidence was inadmissible in any criminal proceedings except for proceedings under the ICAC Act.

My story bears a striking resemblance to the testimony of one of inmates at the inquiry. This is my version of events.

Saxon approached me, "I've been talking to your brother, do you think you can get me out of here?

"You haven't got enough money!" was my cheeky reply.

Saxon had a gift sent to my wife. Luana was surprised but kept quiet about it. I'd trained her well. On 23rd December 1992 she bought a Holden Commodore from Ray Lahood Motors Pty Ltd for $20,500.

Saxon bragged that he could depend on the help of prison officials holding important positions within the prison system but I didn't trust anyone I did not know personally especially Saxon's 'friends' at the top. They were just as likely to feed you to the wolves, so I refused to help Saxon with any plan other than my own.

My plan was beautiful in its simplicity. One of my duties was to collect laundry from both wings at the Remand Centre every Tuesday morning. I noticed that on most occasions which ever officer was driving the laundry van was in the habit of driving further down the complex to the cafeteria instead of taking the laundry directly to the MRP. The reason the officer would drive to the cafeteria was to pick up bacon and egg rolls for himself and other officers working at the Remand Centre.

I arranged for civilian clothes to be smuggled into the prison. A visitor took the clothes into the toilet, leaving them in the toilet bin. The cleaner, for a sum, collected the clothes during the course of his work.

Plan A was for Saxon to be concealed in a bundle of laundry. On reaching the cafeteria, I was to bribe the van driver to drive out through the boom gates to buy some smokes from a local shop. I would go into the shop with the driver and create a disturbance by knocking over a milkshake giving time for Saxon to make good his escape.

Plan B was in the event of the driver not passing through the boom gates, armed men waiting in a van outside the prison would shoot their way in to take Saxon out.

The inmates staged a couple of dry runs, tying Saxon up in a sheet and covering him with laundry before lifting him onto a trolley. At the time I had been lent a video camera from the governor which he had been using to make a video to take to schools to deter potential offenders.

Ironically, the camera was also used to film the mock escape. It was important to the plan that the right officer should be driving the van, one that would not take too much notice of what was going on.

As it turned out I was released from Long Bay before the escape date so other inmates helped Saxon implement my plan. Saxon, dressed in civvies, was folded up in a sheet and placed in the van with the rest of the laundry. Although the driver was not the one the inmates had expected, they proceeded with the escape.

When the van driver entered the prison cafeteria the prisoner on laundry duty whispered to Saxon, "Go, go, go," and Saxon simply walked through the boom gates and out of the prison where I was waiting with two vehicles. The first was a van carrying arms in case of a shoot-out but it was not needed. Saxon was picked up and driven to a house in Newtown and that was the last time I saw him.

On 1 March 1993, Cargill was rostered to do the 26 post van driver's job for 2 March 1993. His evidence was that he had rarely, if ever, filled this job prior to that date and that he had only done so on a total of four occasions. Cargill testified he not noticed any irregularities in the loading of the laundry van and had indeed left the van unguarded when he entered the cafeteria.

Steven Schiele was working as the officer-in-charge of the MRC gatehouse on 2 March 1993. He never checked the van as he believed the loading of the laundry van was adequately supervised by the laundry van driver. Correctional Officers Robert Hocking and Cameron McKenzie were on duty at the boom gate at the relevant time. They were busy checking cars and vans and assumed anyone in civilian clothes was entitled to leave the jail.

The Commission found the evidence of the three inmates, plus that of Saxon and Cargill unreliable. The Commission's report also stated that there was no support for finding corrupt conduct on the part of any public official.

"That is not to say there was no corrupt conduct; rather, the evidence does not permit a conclusion that there was such conduct by any identified person." The commission's final summation was, "On all the material currently available to the Commission, the 26 Post laundry van presents as the probable, indeed most likely, mode of Saxon's escape. Regrettably, it is a conclusion that cannot be stated with a greater degree of certainty."[1]

Readers will have to draw their own conclusions.

......

1. www.icac.nsw.gov.au/files/html/Fifth_report.htm *Investigation into the Department of Corrective Services, Fifth Report: Two Escapes:*

21

—————

GUILTY OR NOT GUILTY?

Gerry Webb, employed as Detective Sergeant in the Australian Police Force from 1984 to 1993, now works for Corrective Services as a temporary court security officer.

"I would never have agreed to talk to you if Charlie was still offending," he said to the author when asked for an interview for this book, "but he's okay now, keeping out of trouble."

The prosecution had a number of court cases pending, concerning me and my brother, perhaps seven altogether. Gerry thought the Crown's strongest case was breaking and entering into Kempsey Motor Registry Office located at that time in South Street, South Kempsey. He advised the Crown to run this trial first but they did not agree and some other trials preceded it.

Gerry claimed that I, my brother Ralph, Lawrence Donahue and possibly another accomplice broke into the Registry on a Saturday night. We were arrested, interviewed and charged with the break-in. Gerry does not remember interviewing us but testified Ralph and I would never say anything. Police would have accepted bail but in this case no bail was granted and we were placed in cells. In those days the case appeared before the district court within a couple of days, at Kempsey or Port Macquarie where bail could be granted or refused.

As no bail was granted on this occasion we were kept in custody. Lawrence pleaded guilty to the charge and became one of the prosecutor's key witnesses. Lawrence's girlfriend was another witness. Lawrence and his girlfriend testified they had met with the rest of us to plan the crime at the Tavern Hotel (now known as the Macleay Hotel) on the Friday before the break-in. Lawrence's girlfriend said she did not want him to have any part in the affair. On the night of the robbery she was standing at the intersection opposite the Motor Registry and saw us go in. In addition two police officers claimed they saw Ralph and me coming out of the window of the Registry Office.

Gerry's job was to organise the witnesses for the prosecution and appear in court on the day the case was heard. It seemed an open and shut case. The case was tried by a jury of twelve people before judge Bill Hoskings at the Downing Centre in Liverpool Sydney. Witnesses were called in order so Gerry as the last witness in the trial was unable to enter the court until near the end. The verdict was 'not guilty'.

Others, who went in before Gerry, told him they thought Ralph and I intimidated the jury. It was the same result in all seven cases; not guilty. Gerry said he tried to warn the prosecution of what was happening but they did nothing about it. It was frustrating for Gerry, all the work the police did without result.

I don't think it was like that at all. If anyone was intimidating it was the police. They would frighten witnesses by claiming they were in danger if the defendants weren't put away.

In fact, I was not actually involved in the Motor Registry break-in but because the police were always assuming we brothers worked together I was charged along with Ralph.

As both Ralph and I were in the same trial we had twice as many opportunities to challenge the people selected as jurors (twelve challenges instead of six). We challenged any juror we thought would be bad for our case. For example a businessman would not be a good juror so we'd challenge but we'd keep a young Lebanese man as we thought he would have no trouble with us possessing guns. A housewife with kids would be good because she'd understand what our mother had gone through.

Eventually the prosecutor wised up. The last time he acted as prosecutor he promised us if we beat the case he would retire. We were acquitted and with no hard feelings he kept his word and retired.

Gerry is happy to see me doing something with me life.

"Some people don't like Charlie," he said. "Probably because of the flash cars he drives. The yellow Ford he drove when he ran his building company made him stick out like a neon light. People put two and two together and came up with five - some thought he sent the company broke. I trust him more than his brother Ralph; Charlie's more of a thinker."

My longest case went on for years. Tom Morris was stopped by police for speeding. The car was unregistered, Tom was unlicensed and police found marijuana plants in the car. Tom Morris was a marijuana smoker and a drug dealer. He claimed he was speeding to get away from me. Tom claimed I had been up in the bush and had put a gun to his head, telling him to get away from his crop. I was arrested in Kempsey and charged with assault.

"Assaulting who?" I asked quite perplexed.

The police told me the story at the station. Bail was refused and I spent four years on remand before my case was heard. Eventually the case went to court and after one day I was acquitted but I'd spent a lot of time in prison on remand for a crime I did not commit.

I suppose I should consider all the years I should have served but never did but in my mind it was still an injustice.

I never pleaded guilty to any crime. My philosophy was, "If I was at the front of a bank with a gun, smoke coming out of the gun and police caught me with the bag I would still plead not guilty."

You see the system is so crooked. The police and judicial system are only there to make money. They don't really care if you're guilty or not. It's all about negotiation. The Aboriginal Legal Service doesn't really fight for you; they would like you to plead guilty to get a small sentence. We live in a police state. There are so many people in jail on remand waiting for their cases to be heard whether guilty or not. If the police had concentrated on one charge they might have made it stick but there were just so many charges.

Years ago you could do time in jail instead of paying fines at a rate of a day for each $25.00 owed. I always went to jail instead of paying fines. I only actually stayed in a cell at night to sleep. During the day I'd be washing police cars, cleaning or gardening.

The police would come to Bellbrook and find me and ask if I had any money to pay a fine.

"Nup," I'd answer.

"Do you want to cut it out," the police would ask.

"Yep."

I would take a few books with me and the prison time would cut out my fine.

Apart from picking jurors that would help our case Ralph and I would get together to decide what we would say. I'd say one thing and he would say another. The conflicting evidence was confusing. Also, police assumed we both worked together. Once it was proved that I was not at a crime scene the case would collapse.

In one of the seven back to back cases Detective Zane was scheduled to give evidence for the prosecution. The previous night Detective Zane was exposed on the television program *'60 minutes'*, photographed accepting a bribe. The newspaper took up the story the next day. As the prosecution were about to call him to the witness box, my lawyer threw the newspaper onto the prosecution's table. The trail was aborted. I had good lawyers. Due to my notoriety lawyers lined up to take on my cases at no charge.

I ended up spending a number of years in a different jails in New South Wales and Queensland. Once arrested I would face charges of events that had happened months, even years, earlier. Even if I had been acquitted on a charge it looked bad on my record. A large number of offences such as illegal possession of firearms, possession of an unlicensed pistol, stealing, malicious damage, possessing house-breaking implements, resisting arrest and driving in a dangerous manner carried relatively small jail terms but they added up. Most of these crimes were committed while I was on the run avoiding being captured by police. I just would not give up and felt that if I was shot at I was entitled to shoot back.

22

THE ACCIDENT

All through my life I had felt God's presence but had resisted responding.

Late one night I and three mates, James Dunn (Jimmy), Dave Toby and Uncle Bill were travelling from Sydney to Kempsey. It was late and I was tired. I wanted to stop and wait until the next day but Dave had urgent family issues to attend to. Dave fell asleep at the wheel near Freeman's Drive on the freeway not far from Newcastle. The Toyota Prado 4WD left the road, going down a bit of a slope before hitting the safety wire and catapulting into the air. The vehicle rolled six times before coming to a stop, upright, the bonnet resting against the piers of a bridge.

I had been asleep in the passenger seat but woke up as the car rolled in the dust. I stared in unbelief as the car roof crumbled down on me.

In my mind I heard my brother Darren calling, "Wake up Freddie Frog!"

Darren used to call me 'Freddie Frog' after my middle name, Frederick, but Darren had died years ago. Coming to my senses, I squeezed my large frame out of the collapsed passenger window. I called out to the other men but there was no answer. The motor was making a hissing sound and petrol was leaking from the car. Adrenalin pumping, I physically pulled the back door off its hinges and dragged Jimmy out of the backseat, laying him on the ground.

Next I went for Dave. Dave was covered in dust and his legs were stuck between the front console and the steering wheel.

"Leave me, leave me," Dave whispered.

He was a small man but thickset and his legs were bent up. I forced his legs even further toward his chest, pulled him out and laid him out next to Jimmy. Jimmy was sitting up now praying. Uncle Bill got out by himself and was running up and down the road trying to pick up his scattered paperwork. The car was completely crushed. It was a miracle anyone was alive.

An ambulance arrived and shortly after a helicopter landed on the freeway. Dave and Jimmy had broken bones and Dave had cracked ribs as well but Uncle Bill and I sustained no injuries. From then on Jimmy's life changed. He gave his life to Jesus and started attended church. I wanted to follow my friend's example but I was involved with the Dhungutti Bronco Rugby League Club's junior teams which played on Saturday, the day I should be attending church. I knew my reputation actually drew children to the footy field when they should have been at church and felt guilty about it.

After Luana and I were married we had been baptised by Pastor Tulevu at the Kempsey Aboriginal Seventh-Day Adventist Church, but I had not been faithful. The accident should have changed me as it did Jimmy but I resisted God's grace.

Some years later I finally gave in and took my whole family to church. I and my older children attended a youth program in Sydney and Shianna, me, Edward and Ralph all made our decisions to be baptised.

Looking back I can see God working in my life. I should have been dead so many times. I had felt no hesitation in fighting authority or 'putting some-one to sleep' who got on the wrong side of me or hurt my family. I had lived a dangerous, bad life that only I, Neddy and the 'Big Fellow upstairs' knows about.

I accept I will have to answer to God for everything one day. Meanwhile I'm thankful for God's provision for the repentant sinner and I'm trying to live the rest of my life doing something worthwhile and pleasing to my Saviour. God knows I still struggle. At times I can't quite cut my ties to the past but at least I've kept out of jail.

23

LEAKY VALVES

I missed a lot of schooling when I was seven and eight years old because I contracted rheumatic fever. Australia's Aboriginal population suffer the highest incidence of the disease worldwide. Rheumatic fever is a disease affecting the heart, brain, joints and skin and can follow an infection with the organism responsible for `strep throat'; Streptococcus Pyogenes. Dr. Johnson admitted me to Kempsey Hospital where I stayed for months without improvement. When I tried to direct a spoon of porridge towards my mouth it would shake and spill down my shirt. This made staff think I was disabled. I'm not surprised because one in ten patients with rheumatic fever will experience an effect on their nervous system. The condition can lead to a loss of co-ordination and cause involuntary movements in the limbs and face, known as chorea or St. Vitas' dance.

My father, dissatisfied with the medical attention at Kempsey, took me to the public hospital at Armidale. Here physiotherapy treatments affected a cure. One side effect of Rheumatic fever is it can cause thickening and scarring of the heart valves, making them narrower (stenosis) or causing them to leak. It can also affect the pumping power of the heart, limiting its ability to efficiently circulate blood around the body. This type of heart damage is known as rheumatic heart disease. If the damage is severe, surgery may be required to repair or replace the damaged valve and prevent the disease from causing heart failure. In my case rheumatic fever damaged my heart valves.

In early 2007 I was ill with an infection and visited my regular doctor in Bellbrook, Dr. Appleton. Listening through the stethoscope Dr. Appleton found something more serious than an infection. My heart was not making the right sounds. An ultrasound confirmed my heart valves were leaking. A few months later I went for another checkup. This time a cut was made near my hip and a tiny camera inserted into a major artery. I was amazed to watch on the big screen the progress of the camera right up to my heart. Heart surgeon Stephanie Wilson recommended open heart surgery and replacement of both valves because of my childhood disease and the fact that my family on my father's side had a history of heart problems. When my dad died of a heart attack he was only thirty-two years old.

At this time in my life, I was overweight, weighing 130 kg, my blood pressure was high and my sugar was up too. I did not want the operation and decided to prove to the doctors I could get my problem under control by changing my lifestyle. I rang Michael O'Neil, Manager of Misty Mountain, a health retreat in the beautiful mountains at the back of the Five-day Creek area. I participated in a ten day program; three days of juice fasting to clean out my digestive system then 7 days of healthy vegetarian meals plus exercise, massage, water treatments and daily lectures on how to live a healthy life. My weight dropped to 89 kilograms in the following weeks. I came out full of confidence and feeling good about myself.

All my life I'd never taken drugs, smoked or drank and that same willpower helped me follow a strict diet and exercise program for a time. When I went for another check, the specialist was amazed he couldn't hear my heart valves leaking anymore and was surprised by how fit and healthy I looked. Nevertheless, the hospital rang me three times to book an appointment for surgery but I evaded the operation each time, sticking to my healthy regime.

My last check-up took place in Sydney about 8:00 a.m. on the 26th August 2007. My family and I drove to Sydney, staying at an aunt's place in La Perouse close to the hospital. The next day I jogged up the hospital steps. Hospital staff directed me to a bed. A nurse arrived with a razor and asked me to shave my chest. My children were with me so I asked Luana to take them back to La Perouse as it seemed this check up might take a bit longer; I had been asked to stay overnight.

Forms were brought for me to sign. I signed never actually reading them. The following day two doctors visited me.

One asked me, "Do you like dogs?"

I had been tracked by too many dogs to be particularly fond of them so I answered, "Not really, I'm not a dog lover."

"Well," the doctor said, "when we inject this stuff into you, you may have nightmares and you might see dogs attacking you."

"Don't worry," I chuckled, "I'm not scared of the mongrels."

The doctors wheeled me out of the ward.

"Have you ever had an operation before?" one asked.

"Nah, nah, never 'ad an operation," I replied.

My arms were strapped to the bed as they wheeled me into the operating theatre.

Suddenly suspicious, I demanded, "What's going on?"

"You're the first one in today," the anaesthetist said.

"No, no, you've got it wrong. You've got the wrong fella!"

The injection found my vein.

"Where's the doctor? I'm not having heart surgery! Get me a doctor!" I was getting desperate.

By this time Drs. Stephanie Wilson and Paul Jansz had arrived. Amid all the fuss they were debating whether I should have open heart surgery or not. Dr. Wilson was my heart specialist while Dr. Jansz was a visiting cardiothoracic and transplant surgeon from America. Dr Jansz was saying you don't have to fix something that doesn't need fixing but Dr. Wilson was determined to go ahead with the surgery. Defective valves may cause congestive heart failure and infections (infective endocarditis). She knew I had a large family and wanted me to be around for my children.

There were three choices for valve replacement, natural valves are from human donors (cadavers), modified natural valves coming from animal donors, (porcine valves from pigs, bovine from cows) and artificial valves made of metal. Pig valves are similar to those of a human but do not last as long as the artificial valve having to be replaced every sixteen years. The metal valve lasts for life but the patient needs to be on medication to prevent blood clots. I had learnt that the drug used, warfarin (nicknamed 'rat poison') thins the blood so even a casual knock can cause bleeding and the valve is noisy, sounding something like a cat purring.

"Don't put in the metal valves!" were my last words before falling unconscious.

I woke up after what seemed to be only a few minutes later.

My son Freddie was touching me, "Wake up Daddy, wake up!"

The nurse came over to hear me still muttering, "Whatever you do, don't put in the metal valves!"

She went for a doctor. "Don't worry, Mr. Quinlan, we didn't replace your valves, we only repaired them."

My condition had improved so much that the doctors took some tissue from my leg and repaired the heart valves instead of replacing them. Not withstanding, my heart had to be removed from my chest and dissected in two to reach the valves. My heart was out of my body for eight hours.

After the operation I surprised staff by being on my feet within days and walking. Now I have a big cross of scar tissue on my chest to go with all the other scars I have collected.

I've always said, "Aborigines are a fast growing race and a fast dying race."

An Aboriginal family averages 3.5 persons whereas a white family averages 2.6 persons. However the average Aboriginal Australian living in a urban area dies around age 60 years of age (50 in a remote area), approximately 24 years earlier than his white counterpart.[1]

......

1. www.creativespirits.info/aboriginalculture/people/aboriginal-statistic-timeline.html

24

———

LUANA

I was born in Kempsey. My mum home-schooled me for kindergarten then I went to West Kempsey Primary. I was only in Year 7 at Kempsey High for a few months because my Mum and Dad became Christians and moved to Casino to keep their faith strong. After that we moved to Lismore where my father had grown up. He worked for Community Services helping kids when they went to court. We moved around a lot.

I left school after Year 9, when I was fifteen and went looking for a job. It wasn't easy finding a job; but I got one in a take-away shop. It only lasted a couple of weeks because the owner went bankrupt. The owner never paid me but I didn't take her to court as she was pregnant and I felt sorry for her. My sister worked in another take-away shop and I filled in for her sometimes, making sandwiches and milkshakes. Eventually I worked there too. The shop was owned by a lovely old Christian lady. Later I worked at O'Mears Supermarket. They trusted me there even though I was young and Aboriginal. I even made up the pays sometimes.

As far as Charlie goes, it seems I knew him all my life. He was always around our place. My brother Barry (that was his name, but everyone called him by his second name, Mark) hung out with Charlie. They used to steal car parts. Mum wondered where all the parts came from and at the time I didn't understand they were stolen either.

Then Charlie's Dad and my Dad were good mates. Charlie and his brother, Ralph, often used to sleep at our place. He was eleven years older than me. I knew he got into trouble and was in jail a lot but I thought the police were just making it hard for him.

Charlie had lots of girlfriends, and he had already fathered three children. When I was eighteen we fell in love and started living together. I didn't want to have children out of wedlock. I always felt that wasn't right so we decided to get married. Shortly after Charlie had attended the funeral of his baby son he was released from Long Bay Jail. Not long after he was re-arrested and had to serve another few months. We were in love and didn't want to wait, so we were married on November 24th 1992 in Long Bay Goal.

Neither of our parents agreed with the marriage. Charlie's mother disapproved because she felt he should marry the woman he had been living with and by whom he had had two children. However, Charlie reasoned he had children with more than one woman so what was so special about that one. My parents thought I was too young. Why should I marry when I had my whole life before me? Also they were worried about the eleven year age gap between us.

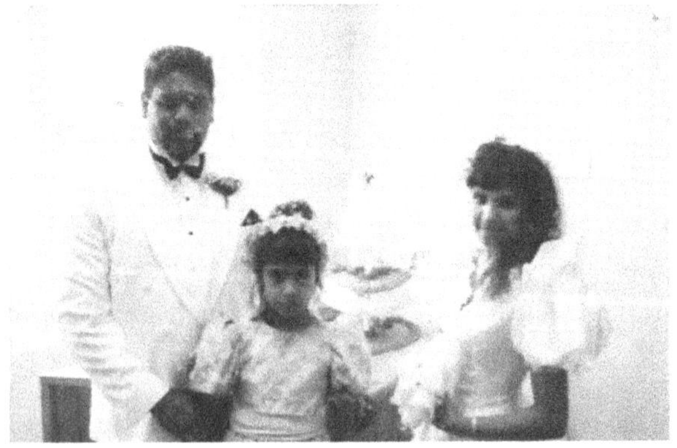

Charlie and Luana's wedding with daughter Amanda in Long Bay Gaol

So our parents did not come to the wedding. My uncle, Harold Smith, gave me away. Charlie's daughter Mandy was our flower girl. Charlie's brother Ralph was in the same jail as Charlie so he was there with his girlfriend. I hired a beautiful white dress. It was from America and I was the first to wear it, though it cost hundreds of dollars and it was only for a few hours.

We weren't allowed much in the jail but the screws bought us a wedding cake. After the ceremony we all sat down to cake and sandwiches before Charlie had to go back to his cell.

Charlie got on well with the screws and the governor. He used to talk to other prisoners when they threatened suicide. When a prisoner hung himself Charlie would cut them down. The screws didn't like to do that.

I didn't know much when I was first married. On the day of our wedding one girl rang to tell Charlie not to go ahead with the wedding! She was the mother of one of his children. Of course, I knew nothing about it 'til later.

As it turned out, the next year when I was in hospital having our first son, Charlie, Eileen, Charlie's old flame, came into the hospital at the same time. I couldn't wait to get out of there as I was scared she was going to hurt little Charlie. We looked after Charlie's other children from time to time. I felt sorry for them, especially little Edward. One day, at a footy match Eileen came up to Charlie and gave him Edward. He was a pathetic sight covered with scabs and had bad ears. Charlie's sister Michelle took him for a while, and then we kept him.

I eventually found out that Charlie was still visiting Eileen in Sydney for a year after our marriage. Everyone knew but me. I still don't understand why no-one told me. I was hurt and angry and did some foolish things; started drinking and had an affair. Charlie beat me up a couple of times over that. One of the silliest things I did was to form a close friendship with Eileen for a time.

I've left Charlie a few times but always came back. Charlie and I have ten children now. Little Charvez is only a few months old and that's the last one. Things are a lot better now, we go to church and Charlie stays at home more. Some things still annoy me, like the time Charlie sold my car to buy football jerseys for the team. Charlie helps the local football team; he's mad about footy.

He used to buy cars at the auctions and still does for people who need a car and hands out money to anyone who needs it even more than to his own kids. I don't know where the money comes from and I don't want to know.

25

TEARS IN THE RAIN

Over ten years in and out of different jails had an effect on my thinking. I used to blame others, my mates, my family, the police and the screws for my problems but now I admitted my situation was of my own making. I had come to the realisation that it was pointless trying to beat the system, the system always won in the end.

With the help of other inmates I wrote and directed the making of a video, entitled 'Tears in the Rain" shot on location in Long Bay Correctional Centre. The video depicted life in 'segregation', unable to talk to anyone, alone in a cell with a cement bed, one pillow and a blanket, the surveillance camera watching the prisoner's every move. Days were long and boring. An inmate could end up in segregation for playing up or fighting.

In jail, I was a number; twelve-sixty-twenty-four. When I first went to jail there were fewer Aborigines detained and mostly for minor offences like stealing cars. Now many young Aboriginals were in jail on more serious charges such as armed robbery and murder.

The video depicted a typical visit of the Aboriginal Legal Advisor. Visits took place shortly before the inmate's court case. The prisoner was encouraged to apply for bail but no-one had any money for bail or for a private solicitor. I was always in handcuffs for lawyer's visit because of nature of my offences. The Aboriginal Legal Advisor would often recommend the prisoner plead guilty even if he was innocent of the crime to secure a 'light' sentence. The video was intended to make young people think seriously about their future.

For a few months the prison ran a program in the Primary and Secondary Schools. It was like a regular class, I would talk about my experiences as a prisoner, then the Correctional Officer would speak about what it was like to work in a prison. I would give a graphic account of my experience of a trip in a police wagon.

"You're thrown in a meat wagon handcuffed to another prisoner, if it's hot, the air conditioner will be switched off, if it's cold, the cops turn it on full blast."

At the end of the talk the students had opportunity to ask questions. The most common question was about the possibility of getting raped or stabbed.

Violence was and is an all too real possibility in prison. The public are generally unaware of the extent of prison violence. During the years I spent at Long Bay Jail violence was common. A video can be viewed on U-tube[1] showing a full-scale brawl between Asian and Aboriginal inmates. How the video filmed by surveillance cameras in the jail ended up on you tube is unknown. Both I and my brother, Ralph were present. I was wearing a white cap and not actively attacking anyone but defending himself from a man attempting to stab me with a shiv.

A shiv is a knife made in the prison made from a sharpened toothbrush and capable of causing death. An Asian prisoner can be seen catapulting himself through the air landing on Ralph's back with both feet. Ralph is actively fighting. He and two other men retaliate on an Asian inmate who is later taken to hospital.

The prison warders are courageously trying to break up the fight but are ineffective. However their presence prevents anyone from being killed until the MEU (Malamar Emergency Unit) arrive and restore order. The worst part is the retaliation behind the scenes in the ensuing weeks. The man who tried to stab me was dealt with. You had to be known as fearless to survive in jail.

More recently the Sunday Telegraph published an article entitled, 'Shots fired in covered up prison brawl.' Concerning a brawl in Long Bail Jail[2] Police reporter, Yoni Bashan writes 'The incident was kept under wraps by the Department of Corrective Services (DCS) until enquires by *The Sunday Telegraph*. Privately, DCS officials have described the riot as the "worst in 25 years."'. The article states, 'Up to 80 prison guards were needed to stop the fighting last Tuesday when violence erupted between up to 40 Middle Eastern and Aboriginal prisoners.' 'The prisoners, some from maximum security, used gym weights to savagely beat each other and officers, during the melee, which lasted up to half an hour. The assistant commissioner played down the incident but the prison officers saw it differently describing the situation to *The Sunday Telegraph* as "straight out of a movie" and "extremely frightening". 'Inmates known to have been involved include members of the violent street gang Notorious and its Muslim Brotherhood Movement (MBM) offshoot. Notorious has had a surge in membership inside the prison system through coercion and standover tactics with at least 200 members in State jails.'

In 1990 I and my brother Ralph started up an organisation called *Brothers-in-Arms* primarily to protect Aboriginal inmates. It was a source of income but more importantly a way of protecting each other. The organisation originally had 575 members and still exists today as half of the original members are still in prison including my brother Ralph.

*Brothers-in-Arms' i*s styled on the African-American organisation the *Black Panther Party*' Originally titled the *Black Panther Party for Self-defense* the party was established to promote black power and self-defense through acts of social agitation. It was active in the United States from the mid-1960s into the 1970s. Founded in Oakland, California, by Huey P. Newton and Bobby Seale on October 15, 1966, the organisation initially set forth a doctrine calling for the protection of

African American neighbourhoods from police brutality, in the interest of African-American justice. The Black Panthers ultimately condemned black nationalism as "black racism".

Later the party became more focused on socialism without racial exclusivity instituting a variety of community programs to alleviate poverty and improve health among communities deemed most needful of aid. The group's political goals were often overshadowed by their confrontational and militant tactics and by their suspicions of law enforcement agents. The Black Panthers considered them as oppressors to be overcome by a willingness to take up armed self-defense.[3]

During my internment at Long Bay, all types of racism existed behind bars; some black prisoners were anti-white and some white prisoners were anti-black. The Aboriginal prisoners held the balance of power in prison mainly due to superior numbers and at least while I was interned owing to my leadership and organisational skills.

On the outside gangs such as the bikies, Commancheros and the Bandidos, and the Bra Boys were feared. The Bra Boys were an Australian surf gang founded and based in Maroubra, an eastern suburb of Sydney, New South Wales who achieved notoriety in the 1960's through violent clashes with members of the public and police. Inside these gangs held no power and often needed protection themselves.

Brawls between rival fractions were ignited by the competition for power and prison territory. In the 1900's conflict was mainly between Aboriginals and Whites or Aboriginals and Asians. Today the Lebanese and Aboriginals are the main players.

Brothers in Arms while maintaining its original purpose has become a more militant organisation expanding its influence to the Sydney Suburbs dominated by immigrants and Aboriginals. Aboriginals claiming for land rights are also taking a more militant position fuelled by the large Aboriginal population in prison.

Although I have been a free man for over 10 years I still have people ask me for help to protect Aboriginals going to jail.

On a trip to Redfern, Sydney in November 2001 I became involved in an altercation between a group of young Aboriginals and a Lebanese family. The Lebanese man, who owned a carwash business, and his family had been threatened and intimidated by the young Aboriginals who were claiming the business as 'their' territory. The situation was tense when I entered the house.

I approached the owner of the carwash, "Let's talk this over, the boys are in the wrong here."

"There's no point," he said, "The boys will only be back again, might as well give them the business. My mum can't take any more of this."

Indeed, the older woman was cowering in the corner of the room, terrified.

"Let me talk to her," I suggested.

"She won't talk to you," he insisted.

Nevertheless I approached the woman and gently took her hand, "I'm sorry M'am, the boys are out of line, I promise it won't happen again."

She smiled at me, softly saying, "Thank you, thank you."

Seeing his mother pacified, the car wash owner agreed to met with me at a later date. With some difficulty I persuaded the boys to leave.

Later we talked. "My business isn't doing well, might as well give it to them," the Lebanese man said.

"No," I relied, "I've got a plan. How about hiring an Aboriginal man to manage the business?"

"What!"

"Show them we can work together. Within this area there are many Aboriginal organisations, Health Clinics, Housing....... They'll get their cars washed at your carwash. I'll visit the police stations and tell how you are all working together and they'll bring their cars to you too."

He promised to follow my advice and kept his word. The police were amazed and promised to support the proposal. In a small way I'm trying to prevent problems but I forecast an explosion of trouble in the future.

Many friends and relatives stood by me when I was released from prison. At first police followed me everywhere, to the point of harassment. It was almost as if they were determined to make me commit a crime. I feel I have endured discrimination all my life.

A recent example is the case of my cancelled licence. In 2008 I lost my licence for three months after loosing too many points. I still had possession of my licence dated 2011 and was driving on it thinking it was valid after the three months was up. In 2010 I was stopped by a traffic policeman not for any infringement but well, it's what you expect if you're a black fella driving a truck.

I showed the police my licence and was informed my licence had been cancelled and I had not renewed it. The case went to Balmain Court. I sat there from 9:30 in the morning 'til 4:30 in the afternoon. My case was the last to be called up. I listened to the case before. A nineteen year old white girl on her P plates who'd been caught drink driving over the limit. She was fined $500.00 and was allowed to keep her licence.

I represented himself and explained the misunderstanding. My licence was cancelled for twelve months.

"This is outrageous," I told the judge, "are you a racist toward Aboriginal people or just ignorant."

The lady acting as the prosecutor on his case advised me to appeal.

I don't let racism get me down. I've been a fighter all my life and it's a matter of pride to me that despite all the harassment the police couldn't break me. Now I count many of my former police 'enemies' as friends.

....

1. http://www.youtube.com/watch?V=Bxl7i24fbo8 Asian vs Aboriginal Prison Brawl Australia sighted 15.12.09

2. The Sydney Morning Herald, November 29, 2009, *Shots fired in covered up prison brawl*, police reporter Yoni Bashan

3. http://en.wikipedia.org/wiki/Black Panther Party sighted 29.12.09

26

LIFE AFTER PRISON

While in Cessnock Correctional Centre I organised a Rugby League team. I wasn't a player, more like a manager. The team was called the Cessnock Devils. Approved by the Governor the team would train in the afternoon after their work duties. Uniforms were purchased by the Prison and the team played in the local competition. The men were driven to the venue on a bus accompanied by guards, unarmed but equipped with walkie-talkies. On their return the inmates's urine was tested for drugs. None of the inmates ever tried to escape because they knew that would mean a stint in segregation or being sent to another jail with no hope of playing on the team again.

When I was serving time in Long Bay Correctional Centre I organised another team. This time the prisoners were not allowed to play outside the prison but teams such as the Manly Sea Eagles and North Sydney Bears came to play them. The jail had a well maintained oval within its walls. The inmates even played against first grade players and after the game could have a photo taken with the star players. I reckoned that playing football was a way to reduce the number of stabbings in the jail. Stabbings were common, a sharpened toothbrush could be fatal and inmates were fighting simply because of boredom. Training and football games gave inmates something to do and a sense of belonging to a team.

Once out of prison my energies were directed in ways to keep me from criminal activities. I reasoned football would help young Aboriginals to keep off the streets and reduce crime in their communities. Football could be a venue for Aboriginals to form positive relationships with the wider Australian community and promote health. I was president of NSWRL (New South Wales Rugby League Association) for four years.

On the Labour Day long weekend this organisation holds the biggest tournament of Aboriginal teams in the state, known as the 'Knock-out'. Sixty-two teams of all ages and women's teams too play for the trophy. The following year the competition would be held at the home town of the club that won the most games. The 'Knock-out' was formed with the view to providing a stage for the many and very talented Aboriginal country footballers who had been overlooked by talent scouts due to racism and lack of country-based recruitment. The whole idea was about more than winning a football competition. It was about family, about community and about getting people together for fun and celebration.

In conjunction with Moving Mountains Pty. Ltd. (a registered training organisation) a Strategic Plan 2007-2010 was established to formalise Aboriginal participation in Rugby League and other sports and to help address community issues facing the Indigenous population. The report cited statistics that needed addressing. In 2004, 67% of Indigenous students did not finish secondary education and 23% of Indigenous people were unemployed. The Australian Bureau of Statistics 2000 tables 1727.4 Indigenous people were imprisoned per 100,000 compared to the general rate of 146.7 per 100,000. Indigenous people were 17.3 times more likely to be imprisoned, 14.7 times more likely to be arrested and 16.5 times more likely to die in custody.[1]

For many years I was President of the Dhungutti Broncos Rugby League Football Club. The club is the first Aboriginal Rugby League club to play under the Country Rugby League Association. Jimmy Anderson, an ex-police officer, was in the forces when I was on the run but now we meet around the same table. Jimmy was the Secretary Registrar of Group 2 Rugby League and President of the Bellingen

Football Club. There are 10 teams in the competition. Their first major tournament took place over Easter 2009 at the Verge Street sports complex in Kempsey, a strictly drug and alcohol free event. The highlight of the event was Bronco's star player, Greg Inglis, running a coaching clinic on Friday.

When I meet with the committee I talk using white man's law. An example is an issue that arose concerning some boys who signed up to play with Dhungutti Broncos but later wanted to play for another team. The boys had accepted sponsorship money from a white businessman. I explained to these boys that signing a sponsorship deal commits them to the club or if they really want to switch clubs they must return to money to be used to attract another player.

While in prison I qualified as a National Parks and Wildlife Ranger. I thought my qualifications and my knowledge of the bush eminently suited me for life as a ranger. When I was released I had an interview at the Port Macquarie office. The job required me to carry a pistol. This was disallowed because of my criminal record so that certificate did me no good at all; it's just gathering dust in the bottom drawer of my desk.

When a cousin suggested we open a cafe in Kempsey I agreed. It wasn't a success. Customers would often put the cost 'on tab' and then never pay. I gave away food for free much too often and hired too many young kids who needed work to keep off the streets. So we closed.

Not one to be discouraged and always ready for a challenge I started up a building company, the *'Thungutti Estate Housing Company'*, Australia's first Aboriginal building company. I secured a contract from the Australian Government to repair and build Aboriginal houses. At its height my company employed 75 persons. The main aims were to provide employment for Indigenous people especially youth to be apprenticed in the various building trades. Government helped by allowing tax free purchases of materials and vehicles.

The company eventually closed and I felt the Aboriginal people had let me down. Under the 'Sunset Clause' all the money was allocated to the Aboriginal Land Councils and Communities in New South Wales for repairs and construction. The company required new construction as well as repairs to provide enough employment for its workers and experience for the apprentices. Despite some of the committee members having family members even sons and daughters working for Thungutti Estate Housing Company money and contracts were withheld.

I needed $150,000 to cover operational costs until the next payment arrived. I was asked to leave the room while the committee debated the request. The answer was no. I had to start sacking employees. A government man named Smith was sent from Centrelink encouraging the workers to leave and go back on Centrelink payments and it got political until the government withdrew the funding.

I think the whole affair was sparked by jealousy. I'd say the Aboriginal people are the most jealous race in the world. If white men want to destroy us just put a bucketful of money down and leave the room. A few months later I went to Sydney. My white mates asked him me why I didn't talk to them. They would have bankrolled me. It was too late so I put the whole enterprise behind me.

While in prison I became a spokesman for Aboriginal prisoners. Fightings and stabbings mostly happened because the prisoners were bored. I convinced the Governor to allow the prisoners stereos, earphones and television so the prisoners could listen to music and stories. I studied a bit of law and politics through TAFE. On my release I ran unsuccessfully for membership of ATSIC (Aboriginal and Torres Strait Islander Council) and in 2007 campaigned for the New South Wales Aboriginal Land Council. There is an election every 3 years for a position on the council, 12 people being elected from different regions of New South Wales. I only had three weeks to campaign. I campaigned as a 'strong' voice, 'a new millennium', 'a new man' and narrowly missed being elected by a few votes to Bev Manton. New elections are coming up in 2010 and I reckon Bev is worried.

I've been spending more time than usual in Sydney. I've started another building company. All those people I've 'minded' and others I've helped over the years, it's all come back to me now. Much of my business in the past was protecting high profile people in the corporate world, wealthy business men and women and politicians. This activity was legal except for my 'partner', my pet name for the gun I always carried on him.

"You can't go to war without your sword," I'd say.

One of these men is businessman, Ian Lazar. I met Ian about 20 years ago. Ian was instrumental is influencing me away from a life of crime and setting me up as a minder. Wealthy businessmen can be a target for standover men. Some years ago two men attempted to kidnap Ian. Realising his danger Ian managed to make just one quick call before being escorted by the two men in the direction of Double Bay wharf in Sydney. That call was to me. Fortunately I was in the vicinity with my business partner Dave. I raced the vehicle to the area and spotted the three men walking quickly through a park.

I walked right up to them and put my arm around Ian's shoulder.

"You're coming with me." I said.

"No, he's not," one of other two replied.

I lifted my shirt slightly to reveal my gun and nodded my head towards a vehicle in the distance.

"There's coppers about."

Indeed there was a car of undercover police not too far away. I could always sense the presence of police. Ian's potential kidnappers backed off and that was the end of it. Just my reputation and presence gave protection to my clients and they were prepared to pay handsomely for it.

Over the years physical intimidation gave way to negotiation. I could always knuckle but I came to realise that talking it through had a better long term effect. It was through my negotiating skills that my present enterprise came to fruition. Companies as well as private individuals are also targets of the criminal world. In the 1980's a Multiplex construction site became target of intimidation. To force a kickback from the company certain individuals were intimidating the company even to firing on employers working the cranes. I became aware what was happening and had a 'chat' to the management.

"I can sort this out," I said, "it won't happen again."

They were dubious but gave me permission to negotiate with the trouble makers. It was more my negotiation skills than brute force that sorted out that problem.

Many years later, I was doing business with some lawyers when they mentioned that they dealt with *Multiplex* and introduced me to one of the *Multiplex* people. This man not only remembered my help in the past but also had a desire to help Indigenous people. As a result of that meeting, I, as the Chief Executive Officer and the five young Indigenous men who form the board of *United Tribes Building Company* met with *Multiplex* executives and worked out a plan for operation of the company. United Tribes Building Company now has its headquarters in the City Towers building, Park Street Sydney. *Multiplex's* lawyers and accountants have rooms in the same building and have helped me set up the company. Multiplex supplies the contracts, currently a shopping centre in Gosford, a medical centre in Mount Druitt and twenty-five townhouses. The company employs fifteen Indigenous tradespersons and a number of Indigenous apprentices and labourers. One of my sons is an apprentice chippie with the company.

I'd tried so many things to keep myself on the straight and narrow but can't say I've been too successful. A lot of Aboriginal folk don't like me and probably with good reason. I keep myself in money though social security as I have a lot of children and my minder duties for Ian Lazar. Ian's a mortgage broker in Sydney and probably liked less than myself. His business is lending money to people or business that are in financial trouble. Usually the business fails but Ian gets his money.

One day I had an urgent call from Fay Oliver, Principal of Mirriwinni Gardens Aboriginal Academy located east of Bellbrook. I worked at the school for a short time, meeting one of my girlfriends, Robyn Skinner there. It's a beautiful property right on the Nulla Nulla Creek. The school started in a ramshackle building at Five Day Creek, the children being taught by Fay, a registered teacher, one of the few Aboriginal graduates in her day.

Later the school moved to the Nulla Nulla property. Pastor Rosenthal was pastor for the Bellbrook mob at the time and through much prayer and some influential friends the property was purchased miraculously for the Aboriginal people. The boarding school had operated for more than 30 years and educated more than 1500 children but was now in financial difficulty and had been for some time. Government support has been withdrawn. The staff couldn't be paid and most had never received superannuation so one by one they left. In addition the school owed the tax department a huge sum.

The Principal, Fay, was desperate and pleaded with me.

"You know people who could lend us money,' she said, 'Please help us, we've nowhere else to go.'

I warned her about Ian's way of business but she talked to him anyway and subsequently she received no help and the property was forcibly sold in 2009. Now it belongs to Misty Mountain Health Retreat but some of the Bellbrook mob still harbour a grudge against me. They think I sold out the school out but really I was trying to warn Fay. That property should never have been lost to the Aboriginal people and I think the government should have stepped in to stop the sale.

......

1. Aboriginal Australian League Inc. (AAL) Strategic Plan 2007-2010, Moving Mountains Pty Ltd. © 2007.

27

THE FINAL CHAPTER

"Hi Fred, how are you?"

"Uh-uh. How's the book going Auntie Bridget? Have you thought of a good title yet?"

"Maybe *Oker – The Assassin, the story of Frederick Charles Quinlan* or *Against All Odds*. The book is nearly finished Fred, but how are you? The line's bad; I can't hear you well."

"I've been in Sydney for a while. I've got throat cancer."

"What! What did you say!

"I've got cancer of the throat; had it a while now."

"How bad is it?"

"The doctors have given me six months."

My first thought was after all he's been through how could Fred have cancer of the throat, he's never even smoked.

Many months have now passed since that awful diagnosis. Charlie started walking five kilometres every day eating a strict vegetarian diet. He's feeling good. The big green fourteen seater with 'JESUS IS THE

ANSWER' in big bold letters on the back and 'Dhungutti tribe' is a testimony to the world that Charlie is putting his trust in God.

I visited Luana last week. She looked like she'd put on a bit of weight.

"I expecting again," she told me.

"But, Luana, you told me you were going to have the operation," I exclaimed.

"Yeah, I know, I filled in the forms but they were never sent and now it's too late."

On the second of April, 2010 another healthy edition to the Quinlan family came into the world, named Nullawaah Methuselah Rickie Quinlan.

Charlie's cancer's in remission and he's looking as fit as ever.

Fred and Luana were lying on their bed in a rare moment of peace. All the children were with family and they were alone.

"Luana," said Fred, "We've got to completely commit our lives to Jesus. I've been sitting on the fence, just going to church from time to time, sometimes more interested in the footie team than Jesus. Even some of my own children are in jail. What sort of example have I been? I've got to get my priorities right. It's time to get back to where we came from. I'm going to buy land at the Nulla not far from the scenes of conflict years ago when the Thungutti people were fighting for their very existence. I want to go home. We'll build a place for the kids. It'll be like a dormitory style with places for friends and relatives to stay."

Sadly that dream never came to pass.

Some years later, Fred developed a seeping hole in his foot. It wasn't healing so he went to Kempsey hospital and was admitted. The doctors told him they would have to amputate his foot.

"You have a diabetic foot ulcer and if we don't amputate it will spread to the rest of your leg."

Fred had been a fit, active man all his life and the thought of missing a foot was too much. He refused to stay in hospital, discharged himself and went home. The foot didn't heal and again he was admitted. By now the whole leg was affected and Fred's leg was amputated from the hip down. The gangrene was not halted and he was going downhill rapidly. His past rose up before him and on the 15th May 2018 the Daily Mail reported;

Former underworld figure offers to lead detective to ten bodies in exchange for immunity as he admits the 15 year secret has 'eaten away at him'.

Charlie Quinlan has revealed he knows where 10 bodies are buried in Australia. The former underworld figure claims to know where Sidney Collins' body is.

The 55-year-old told detectives he would lead them to bodies for immunity Charlie Quinlan has revealed he wants immunity in return for the secrets he has kept for the last 15 years.

The 55-year-old told 7 News he would give police the 'exact location' of 10 bodies including Sidney Collins - notorious Outlaws Motorcycle Club boss who was murdered by Mark 'Chopper' Read in 2002.

"It's been eating at me. Exact location if I'm given immunity. And the families. The families are the main ones but it would be a big relief for me."

He claimed Outlaw's bikie boss Sidney Collins is buried at Tabulam in northern NSW, while the other nine bodies, including two former police officers are buried in the Crookwell area in the state's south.

NSW Police said the details of the deal were still being finalised.

Meanwhile a reporter interviewed Fred while in hospital and the interview was played on National Television. Fred offered to name corrupt police and underworld figures. He also wanted his brother Ralph released from prison as a trade-off.

This put Fred and his family is a precarious position. Fred's whereabouts became a secret known only to hospital staff, police and a few family and friends.

But it was all too late. Charlie's secrets went with him to the grave. Frederick Charles Quinlan, formerly one of Australia's most wanted me, aged 55, died the next day.

Before he died, other secrets of his past plagued his mind. He confessed to the rape of the white girl that day behind the Woolworths building in Kempsey. The reader may form their own opinions about his sincerity but in the end God is the judge.

Fred's funeral was held in the Kempsey Adventist Church. The church was packed with over 100 people. Amongst those who spoke about his life were some of his children and even a representative from the NSW police force.

Following the service he was buried in Thungutti land at Bellbrook cemetery. It had been a long struggle but against all the odds he'd eventually succeeded in a white man's world not by becoming 'white' but by using his native abilities to carve out his family's future in Australia while maintaining his heritage. He was now home at last.

APPENDIX: ABBREVIATIONS AND WORD MEANINGS

JAG Juvenile Aid Group

MRC metropolitan remand centre – area where prisoners were kept while they awaiting for court cases to be held

CIP Central Industrial Prison – prisoners who had been sentenced but were waiting for transfer to another priosn.

MRP – metropolitan remand prison– where prisoners were kept who had been sentenced

Abo – slang for aboriginal

gandhibal – aboriginal word for police

copper – policeman

high profile prisoner- prisoner needing protection or interned for serious offences

Koori – Aboriginal person

meat wagon, wagon – police vehicle for transporting prisoners

nigger – racist term for a black person

sergeant in arms - war leader of a biker group

segregation – area of cells in which extremely dangerous prisoners or prisoner needing protection were placed

screw – prison warder

Thungutti – Charlie's Indigenous tribe, which can also be spelt Dhungutti or Dhangatti

FAMILY HISTORY

<u>Judith and Ralph Quinlan's children in order of birth</u>

Charles Frederick Quinlan born 29.09.62

Sharon Gaye 6.12.63

Darren Earl 28.7.65

Michelle Anne 8.12.66

Ralph Reynold 11.9.68

Jennifer Joan 29.9.69

Lena Irene 24.7.71

Berryl Grace 1.7.73

<u>Charlie's women and children in order of birth</u>

Maria – daughter Bianca

June – son Bradley

Robyn – daughter Amanda : Manda, Mandy - nicknames for Amanda

Cindy – daughter Kylie (Kylie and Amanda are about the same age)

Judy – daughters Virginia and Emily

Eileen – son Charles Dylan (deceased), daughter Tulla and son Edward

His legal wife Luana – and children in order of birth son Charles Frederick, daughters Shania, Shianna, Shuarna, sons Blade, Njaree, Freddie, daughter Tarquita, sons Darren and Charvez

ACKNOWLEDGMENTS

Acknowledgements from the Author

Foremost I acknowledge Charlie for the countless hours he spent talking with me. Also his wife Luana, for her story and looking after the children while Charlie and I were working together. Charlie's mother, Judith Quinlan, whose story led me to delve deeper into the conflicts between the white settlers and her and tribe, the Thungutti people. To Lena, who was prepared to bare her soul. To many others who were willing to share their knowledge and stories, Elva MacKay and her son Rodney Mackay, Eileen Reilly, Eileen Murray, Ralph Quinlan, Neddy Smith, Darryl Wright, Gerry Webb, Paul Davis, James Ball and Ian Lazar among many others. To the Kempsey Historical Society volunteers and library staff in Sydney, Kempsey and Port Macquarie who helped me track down newspaper articles and historical books. To Mary Federow who read the raw manuscript and made corrections and excellent suggestions.

To Jesus Christ, my Lord and Saviour who inspired me to write the book, and who never gave up on Charlie. Only eternity will tell the intervention of God in Charlie's life to keep him alive until he finally turned his back on his life of crime and committed the keeping of his soul to His precious Saviour.

This book is dedicated to the Thungutti people whom I have come to love and admire.

Acknowledgements from Frederick Charles Quinlan

To my mother and best friend, Judith Quinlan nee Holten.

To my father, Ralph Quinlan, Billy Holten, Mum's brother and Jenny Holten, Mum's sister.

To my grandfather Charlie Holten, who taught me so much about the bush and my ancestors.

To Dorothy Cawdwell (nee Quinlan) who was like a mother to me.

To May Kelly, Grace Close and Roy Cook of the Bellbrook. Community, all of whom had a positive influence on me as a young man.

To Pastor Frank Saunders, a good man. He was an Indigenous SDA pastor married to a white woman. He always had an answer from the Bible to all my questions. He would sit down with us prison inmates and listen. A reformed alcoholic he always said, "God picked me up from nothing and he'll do the same for you."

To Pastor George Quinlan.

To my brothers and sisters, Sharon, Darren, Michelle, Ralph, Jennifer, Lena and Berryl.

To my cousin Dave Toby.

To my Uncle Carl Quinlan.

To Stan Murray, Ralph Carl Quinlan, Geoffrey Vale Brown.

To my nephew Paul Davis. He was footy player at the time I was finally released from prison. He came up to me and put $500.00 in my hand. I've never forgotten it.

To those people associated with me and helped keep me out of trouble after I married Luana and was realised from prison.

I thank God for my mother and father; my father for teaching me and my siblings work and responsibility and my mother for teaching us love, honesty, sharing and caring. Over 69 family members have been influenced by their godly lives. So many members of the Thungutti tribe have been an influence on my life for good, resulting in my decision to accept Jesus as my Saviour and to teach my family to do the same.